NINE CIRCLES

EUROPE'S LEADING KENDOGU SUPPLIERS SINCE 1994

武道具

www.ninecircles.co.uk

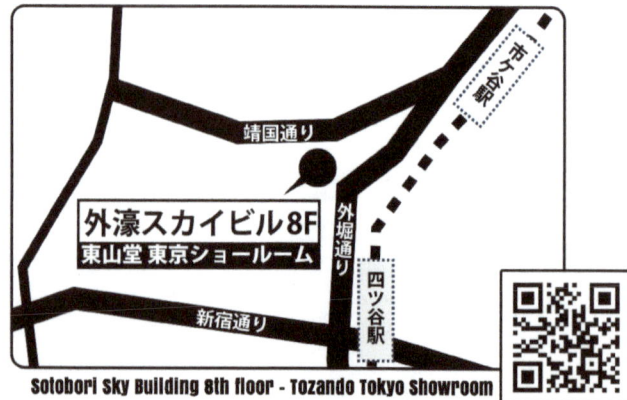

Introducing the Shogun Traveller Bag™ by Shogun Kendogu
a new way for kendoists to travel

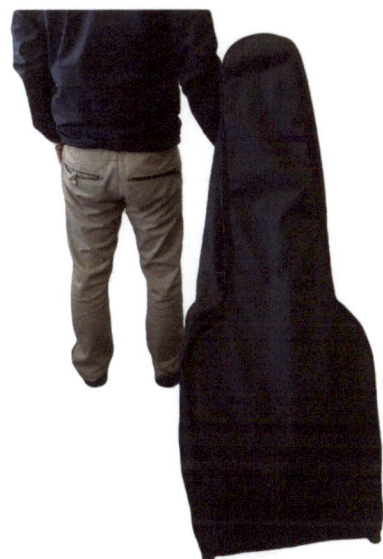

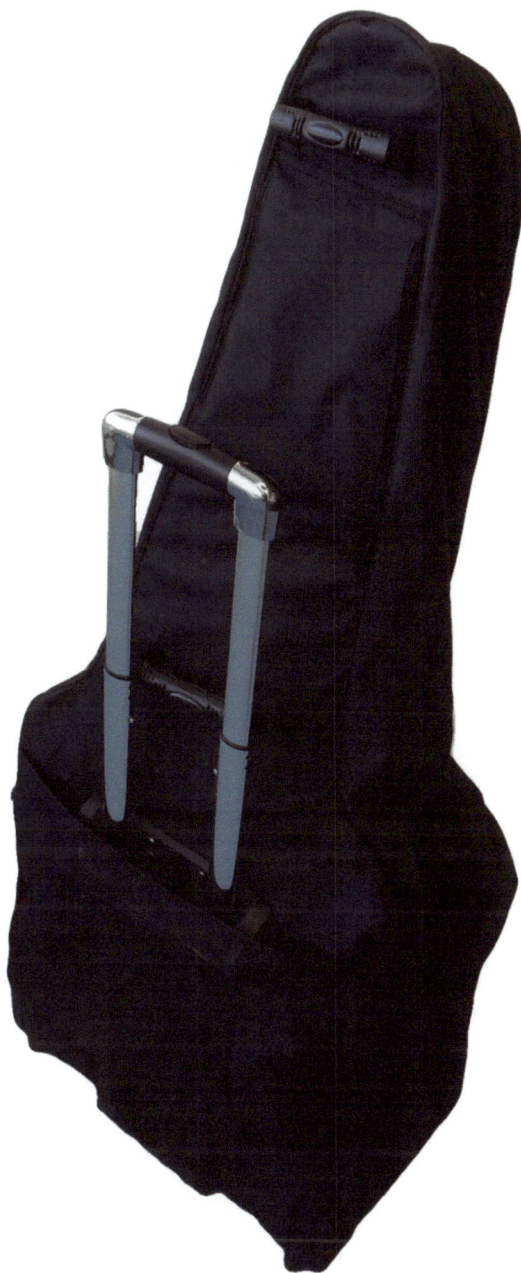

First of its kind, seasoned kendo traveller **Alex Bennett** has teamed up with Shogun Kendogu to create the Shogun Traveller Bag™.

Allowing you to combine your shinai with your other luggage, you can now travel abroad and minimise extra luggage costs charged by many airlines.

If your airline charges extra to check-in more than one item, simply insert your shinai inside the Shogun Traveller Bag ™. If your airline charges more for over-sized baggage, simply roll it down and check your shinai in separately as usual.

Big enough to pack clothes, dōgi, bōgu, and 3 shinai, the Shogun Traveller Bag™ is made with durable yet light weight material.

We have kept the extras to a minimum to ensure the overall weight of your one-piece check-in luggage can be packed with all the necessities and not exceed the specified weight.

RRP US$249
(international shipping included)

Pre-order your Shogun Traveller Bag™ now from www.ShogunKendogu.com and save US$20.

SHOGUN KENDOGU
by katou budougu

KENDO WORLD 16th WKC Special Edition May 2015 Contents

Judging the Judges and "Gross Spectators" _____ 2

Whence art we? _____ 4

The Kendo World (Far Too Brief)
Guide to Tokyo _____ 7

The Not-So-Well-Known History of
International Kendo Competitions _____ 11

History of the WKC 1st–10th _____ 16

Reviewing the History and Challenges of
Women's Participation at the WKC _____ 32

The 11th World Kendo Championships
@ Santa Clara, CA USA March 24–26, 2000 _____ 34

History of the WKC 11th _____ 36

Recollections of Organising a WKC _____ 38

History of the WKC 12th–15th _____ 40

An Examination of *Yūkō-datotsu* Scored
at the 15th World Kendo Championships in Italy _____ 49

The WKC in Graphs _____ 59

The Kendo World WKC Guess Who! _____ 63

Kendo World Staff

•Bunkasha International President & Editor-in-Chief— Alex Bennett PhD
•Bunkasha International Vice President & Assistant Editor—Michael Ishimatsu-Prime MA
•Bunkasha International Vice President & Graphic Design—Shishikura 'Kan' Masashi
•Bunkasha International Vice President—Hamish Robison
•Bunkasha International Vice President—Michael Komoto MA
•Bunkasha International General Manager—Baptiste Tavernier MA
•Senior Consultants—Yonemoto Masayuki, Shima Masahiko

Guest Writers

•Jeff Marsten (Kendo Kyōshi 7-dan, Highline Kendo Club)
•Kate Sylvester (Victoria University)
•Mutō Ken'ichirō (Seikei University)
•Paul Budden (Kendo Kyōshi 7-dan, Kodokan Kendo U.K.)

KW Staff Writers | Translators | Photographers | Graphic Designer | Sub-editors

•Axel Pilgrim PhD
•Blake Bennett MA
•Bruce Flanagan MA
•Bryan Peterson
•Charlie Kondek
•Gabriel Weitzner
•Honda Sōtarō PhD
•Imafuji Masahiro MBA

•Jeff Broderick
•Kate Sylvester MA
•Sergio Boffa PhD
•Stephen Nagy PhD
•Steven Harwood MA
•Stuart Gibson
•Taylor Winter
•Tony Cundy

•Trevor Jones
•Tyler Rothmar
•Yamaguchi Remi
•Vivian Yung
•Yulin Zhuang

KW would like to thank the following people and organisations for their valuable cooperation:

•All Japan Kendo Federation
•E-Bogu
•Eurokendo
•International Budo University

•*Kendo Nihon* Magazine
•Nine Circles
•Nippon Budokan Foundation
•Shogun Kendogu

•TOZANDO
•UC Press
•Zanshin Sports Bar

Editorial Conventions Used in KW Inevitably in a magazine of this nature, many non-English words appear in the text. All Japanese words are italicised and include macrons (ū, ō) etc., apart from common place names and nouns, and words in some captions and headings. As a general exception, KW treats all the martial arts (budo), such as kendo, iaido, jodo, ranks, and so on as Anglicised words without using macrons. Japanese names are written in accordance to the traditional Japanese manner of family name followed by given name. Traditional *ryūha* are written with capitals and therefore are not italicised. 'Kata' with a capital 'K' refers to the set of Nippon Kendo Kata, and *kata* refers to set forms in general. The masculine personal pronoun is used throughout the text in some articles in the interest of readability, and is in no way meant to slight the significant contributions made by female kendoka.

Judging the Judges and "Gross Spectators"

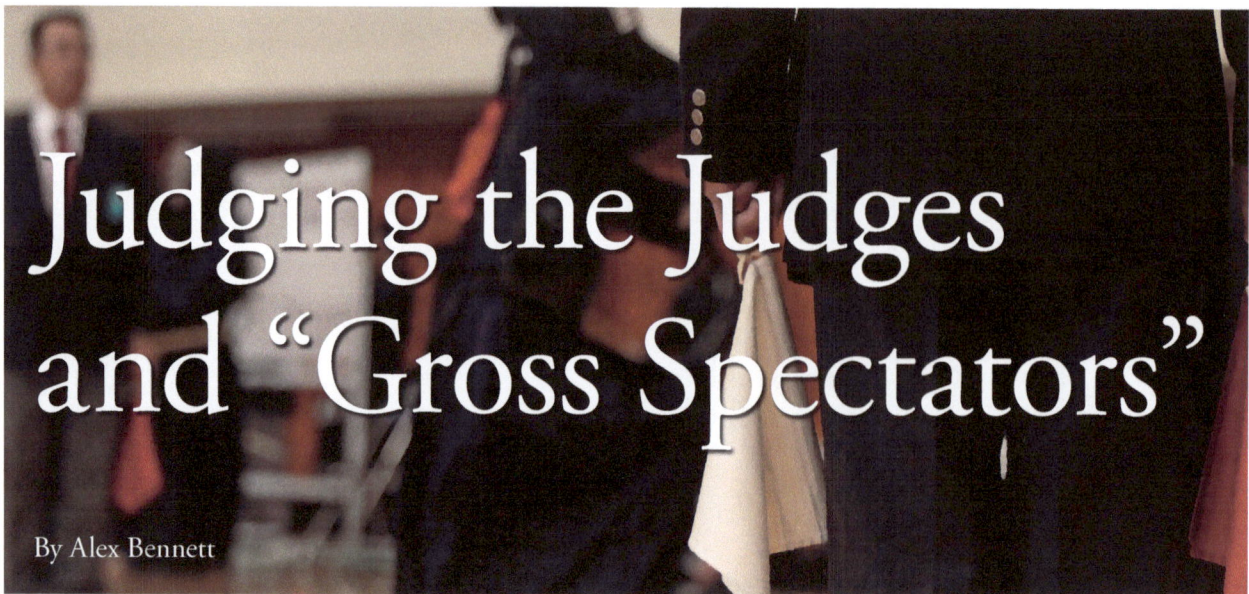

By Alex Bennett

"Remember that when you meet your antagonist, to do everything in a mild agreeable manner. Let your courage be keen, but, at the same time, as polished as your sword."

Richard Brinsley Sheridan (1751–1816)

Fine words by the famous Irish playwright and poet, legendary for the vicious duels he engaged in to defend the honour of his intended wife. Although not as romantic, the world's best kenshi converge every three years to duel-it-out in the quest to take top honours at the WKC. Welcome to Tokyo!

Nevertheless, the issue of *shinpan* quality still continues as a theme for heated discussions. As a *shiai-sha*, I, as have all competitors, experienced calls that should have been given but weren't; and conversely, calls that were given that shouldn't have… *C'est la vie*. After the initial disappointment and feelings of disbelief dissipate into the ether, we hopefully have the maturity to see things from a broader perspective. The negative experience turns into an opportunity for growth as a kendoka, and ideally as a person. Let me explain.

The term for mistaken referee judgments is '*goshin*' in Japanese. After the adrenalin pumping through the veins subsides, one often finds with careful introspection that many of what we perceived as *goshin* were, in actuality, quite hazy. Sometimes the *goshin* is blatant and the manager has the right to appeal, although this rarely happens. More often than not, 'hazy' calls can be attributed to a lack of consistency in one's own kendo. As a *shiai-sha* the onus is on you to convince the referees that a point is valid by creating an opening, and striking with conviction with a unity of mind, body

and technique. You aim for a decisive cut, not a lucky strike. That is the only way to develop one's kendo, and the *shinpan* are charged with facilitating this process.

I have been fortunate to have served as one of the official translators at the FIK & AJKF Shinpan Seminars held before each WKC. The point is always driven home to the world's top *shinpan* in attendance that, "The stars of the show are the *shiai-sha*, and it is the responsibility of the *shinpan* to allow them to fight to the best of their ability, and let them shine on stage knowing that the calls will be impartial and correct." Having worked with all of the WKC *shinpan*, I know only too well how seriously they take the role, and how determined they are to adjudicate to the absolute best of their ability.

It is a thankless job. If the referees get it right, nobody blinks and eye. It was Alex Ferguson who stated, "You can't applaud the referee." On the other hand, if they are seen to get it wrong, the roof inevitably caves in as hordes of people are only too only willing to judge the judges. This trend became disturbingly apparent to me as Kendo World uploaded videos of the 15th WKC on our YouTube site. An unfortunate proportion of the comments left under the match videos chastised the referees for their decisions. Of course, everything is so easy in retrospect, and now with YouTube and modern technology, these matches remain in the public domain to be dissected frame-by-frame for years to come. Given the spectre of eternal infamy, who in their right mind would want to become a *shinpan* in this day and age, at such a high profile event as the WKC?

The role of *shinpan* is a rite of passage. The overall level of *shinpan* dictates how young kendoka will develop. As such, the responsibility of *shinpan* in the continued growth of kendo in their regions or countries cannot be overstated. The fact is, we need good *shinpan* to grow in kendo; and we also need to have experience as *shinpan* to really understand the intangible beauty of our art. *Shinpan* duty is a responsibility of great consequence that we must all perform at some stage in our kendo careers. It provides us with an opportunity in which we can give back some of what we have learned, and ultimately test our understanding of kendo.

Being only human, nobody gets it right all of the time. All we should hope for is that *shinpan* do their best to judge impartially, correctly, and confidently. Failing to do this is unpardonable as a *shinpan*, as a kendoka, and as a human being. This is why *shiai* should not be criticised as running counter to the ideals of budo, but should be cherished as an opportunity for people in all roles to learn and mature. My hat goes off to the *shinpan* at the WKC for their great efforts. I hope that more people in the international kendo community recognise the need to sharpen up their *shinpan* skills and aspire to kendo's ultimate tour-of-duty at future WKCs.

Given we are at the 16WKC, I thought it might be timely to also revisit spectator etiquette. Especially as this topic received a considerable thrashing on the internet and in Japanese kendo magazines after the 15WKC held in Novara, 2012. Those who were there will remember some rather awkward moments in the final of the men's teams—Japan versus Korea. The *shinpan* made their calls, the Korean *senshu* glared at them in disbelief, certain elements of the crowd enunciated their dissonance towards a) *shinpan*, or, b) *senshu*; and many more enunciated their dissonance at the enunciations of dissonance. The result was a confused cacophony of booing and hissing, bolstered by lashings of hooting—an unruly commotion that has no place at a kendo tournament.

Some sports are very strict with crowd behaviour. At golf tournaments, you risk expulsion from the gallery for a poorly timed cough. It is considered jolly bad form to taunt tennis players at Wimbledon, a venue and event which prides itself on exemplary sportsmanship. It is reprehensible, for example, to rejoice a double fault or poor shot. The organisers even promulgated a strict dress and attitude code for spectators in addition to the already long-established players' uniform code. Their precise words were: "No riff-raff please, we're Wimbledon".

With regards to kendo, we are taught that respect for our opponents is of paramount importance given the overtly confrontational nature of what we are doing. We are told to be modest in victory and gracious in defeat. We should never argue with the *shinpan*, irrespective of whether or not their judgments are correct. We are tutored that both winning and losing provides us with clues for developing our kendo, and by extension, our character. Watching the *keiko* or *shiai* of others (*mitori-geiko*) is also a useful means for improvement, so spectating at a tournament is actually a part of our training rather than entertainment.

As such, tournaments are a formal occasion for study, not revelry. Let's take a page out of Wimbledon's book and dress appropriately for the occasion. Let's politely clap a successful result with a mode of decorum and propriety, if there is to be any clapping at all. No cheering *hansoku*, please! And, just as competitors will have an *ippon* rescinded if they insult their opponent or *shinpan*, or let rip with a victory pose, the kendoka in the crowd should surely demonstrate the same self-control, sincerity, and polite manner.

Alas, in Japan I have frequently been witness to cheers of exuberance with the awarding of *hansoku*, and coordinated jeers of 'disapproval' or 'disbelief' to put pressure on the *shinpan* from the safety of the bleachers. Many people also make known their dismay when their team loses the match. Why not be glad to witness a stonking *ippon*, regardless of who the striker is? Of course, nobody WANTS to lose, but isn't the right budo attitude to "keep calm and carry on"—not "carrying on"—once the bout is decided? Then there are those who just up and leave once their team has been eliminated, instead of staying to learn a thing or two from the winning teams. Reprehensible though, are those who just leave their rubbish where they were sitting. This is such a problem in Japan that students are actually finding it difficult to secure venues for their tournaments!

This is not even a matter of spectator etiquette, but more one of common sense. From a kendo perspective though, the way you watch a match is a good indication of your understanding of kendo values. It behoves all of us to keep these things in mind at the 16WKC, and any other tournament. No riff-raff please, we're kendo. To finish as I started, with a quote to ponder…

"Refinement creates beauty everywhere: it is the grossness of the spectator that discovers nothing but grossness in the object."

(William Hazlitt, British writer, 1778–1830)

(This article was adapted from KW 5.1 & 7.3)

Whence art we?

By Alex Bennett

In the hallow'd hall of chivalry, of course. The Nippon Budokan.

Budo was banned for a few years following the Second World War. Incrementally revived as "democratic sports" in the 1950s, budo rose to a high point when judo debuted at the 1964 Summer Olympics in Tokyo. The monolithic Nippon Budokan martial arts hall was constructed in the vicinity of the Imperial Palace in time for the event and became emblematic of the post-war budo renaissance. It was host to the 1st WKC held in 1970 as well, and it is quite a momentous occasion that we can stomp on its sacred floorboards yet again for the 16th WKC. But what of this building, this mecca for modern budo?

Easily recognizable on the Tokyo skyline by the golden onion-shaped dome adorning the roof, the Budokan is known by more people in Japan as the venue for high-profile rock concerts ratherthan budo events (not all Japanese study budo). Several nights a week, budo experts ascend the Kudanshita slope to the Budokan to test their skills in the great dojo located within; but on alternate nights small armies of dodgy scalpers line the same trail, selling illegal concert tickets to legions of eager groupies. Coexistence with the "way of the rocker" is, however, accepted as a necessary evil, for even the almighty Budokan is not exempt from the exorbitant taxes that come with owning 10,830 square meters of prime Tokyo real estate.

The Nippon Budokan building serves as the headquarters for the Nippon Budokan Foundation, which is recognised as the government-endorsed caretaker of budo culture. The following is a timeline of the main events over 50 years of Budokan activities to promote classical and modern budo in Japan and around the world.

Year	Events
1945	GHQ declares a ban on the budo arts.
1961	The Diet Judo Federation is founded. Judo is officially announced as an Olympic event for the Olympic Games to be held in Tokyo in 1964. Initially, a platform was to be installed over the indoor pool in the Yoyogi Sports Hall to serve as the venue. A Diet Member Budo Hall Construction Association is established.
1962	The Nippon Budokan Foundation is born. "Resolution Concerning the Construction of an All-Purpose National Sports Hall" is unanimously passed in the National Diet.
1963	The Olympic Judo venue plan is revised, and it is decided that the yet-to-be-built Nippon Budokan will be the venue. Construction commences in October in Kita-no-Maru Koen, next to the Imperial Palace.
1964	The "Golden Onion" dome is installed on top of the apex on May 12. Copper roofing installation is completed in June, and on September 15, construction of the Nippon Budokan is concluded. The Crown Prince visits the very next day. It took less than a year to complete. About 182,000 personnel were involved in the construction, and costs amount to approximately 1.8 billion yen. The opening Ceremony is conducted on October 3. Following demonstrations of budo (yes, kendo was an Olympic demonstration sport), the first Olympic judo event commences on October 20. On October 23, Dutch judoka Anton Geesink concludes the Olympic competition by defeating the legendary Akio Kaminaga in the final of the Open Weight Division.
1966	1st All Japan Kendo Youth Rensei Training Tournament is held. Those who have been to the Foreign Kendo Leaders Summer Camp held in Kitamoto in recent years will know this as the tournament in which thousands of children fill the main arena each August. Also, the Budo Gakuen School is opened.
1967	*The Nippon Budokan Newsletter* (*Kaihō*) in circulation since 1962 is upgraded to a monthly magazine called *Gekkan Budō*. The World Goodwill Kendo Match is held in cooperation with the All Japan Kendo Federation.
1968	The Japanese Academy of Budo (Nihon Budō Gakkai) is inaugurated and holds its first research convention.
1970	1st WKC held at the Nippon Budokan.
1971	The Nippon Budokan Kenshuu Centre is built in Katsuura City, Chiba Prefecture. The centre is close to the International Budo University, and was the venue for the first Foreign Kendo Leader's Seminar in 1975 (now held each year in Kitamoto).
1974	U.S.A. President Ford visits the Nippon Budokan. A budo demonstration is conducted in his honour.
1977	Japanese Budo Association (Nippon Budō Kyōgikai) is formed.
1978	Nippon Budokan President Matsumae Shigeyoshi (founder of Tokai University and the International Budo University) heads a delegation of budo demonstrators to three countries in Europe. This becomes a regular Budokan activity.
1979	The Japanese Classical Budo Association (Nippon Kobudō Kyōkai) is inaugurated with an official ceremony marking the event. Also, a series of 16mm films recording classical budo (*Nihon-no-kobudō*) are produced. Initially ten classical *ryūha* are introduced. In the following ten years, over 88 films are made introducing various *ryūha*.
1984	Led by the Nippon Budokan, the International Budo University is opened. First year admissions number 515 students.
1989	The 1st International Seminar of Budo Culture is held at the Nippon Budokan Kenshuu Centre and International Budo University in Katsuura. The seminar becomes an annual event.
2003	The first Budokan book in English is produced in co-operation with Kendo World. (*Karate My Life* by Kanazawa Hirokazu).
2005	A revision of the English "Budo Charter" is completed, and the "Budo Charter for Young People" is created to commemorate the 40th anniversary of the Nippon Budokan.
2007	Japanese Budo Association Chairman Shiokawa Masajūrō submits a petition to Prime Minister Abe Shinzō to make budo a compulsory subject in junior high school education.
2008	The Ministry of Education, Culture, Sports, Science and Technology (MEXT) announces that from April, 2012, first and second year students at the eleven-thousand junior high schools throughout Japan will all study budo as a compulsory subject at school. "The Philosophy of Budō" is formulated (*Budō no Rinen*)
2009	The official English translations of "The Philosophy of Budo" and "The Budo Charter for Young People" are completed by Kendo World and made public.
2010	Publication of *Budō: The Martial Ways of Japan* (English) to mark the 45th anniversary of the Nippon Budokan. The Kendo World team was commissioned to make the book, and 10,000 copies were distributed worldwide.
2014	Nippon Budokan 50th Anniversary
2015	16th World Kendo Championships!

Nippon Budokan Presidents

1. Shōriki Matsutarō
2. Kawashima Shōjirō
3. Akagi Munenori
4. Matsumae Shigeyoshi
5. Esaki Masumi
6. Sakamoto Misoji
7. Shiokawa Masajūrō
8. Matsunaga Hikaru (since 2009)

Chairmen of the Board

1. Akagi Munenori
2. Anzai Hiroshi
3. Akagi Munenori
4. Tanaka Eiichi
5. Mōri Matsuhei
6. Esaki Masumi
7. Katō Takenori
8. Sakamoto Misoji
9. Matsunaga Hikaru
10. Inoue Yutaka
11. Usui Hideo (since 2009)

Managing Directors

1. Tanaka Eiichi
2. Miura Hideo
3. Yoshii Takeshige
4. Nitō Masatoshi
5. Yamanaka Gorō
6. Tsujihara Hiroichi
7. Kijima Kihei
8. Kataoka Katsuji
9. Aoki Katsuhiko
10. Mifuji Yoshio (current)

Related Organisations and Institutions Established by the Nippon Budokan:

1. Student Budo Club (Gakusei Budō Kurabu)—Established April 1, 1965
2. Japanese Academy of Budo (Nihon Budō Gakkai)—Established February 3, 1968
3. Japanese Budo Association (Nippon Budō Kyōgikai)—Established April 23, 1977
4. Japanese Kobudo (Classical Budo) Association—Established February 17, 1979
5. National Prefectural Budokan Association (Zenkoku Todōfuken-ritsu Budōkan Kyōgikai)—Established May 27, 1981
6. International Budo University—Established April 12, 1984

Government Subsidised Activities

1. Youth Budo Rensei Tournament—Sixty regional "Rensei" training tournaments are held throughout the country, and one large-scale central Rensei tournament including eight divisions is held over a nine-day period.
2. Instructor Training—National instructor training seminars are conducted for judo, kendo, karate and naginata. Regional community budo instructor seminars for judo, kendo, kyudo, sumo, karate, aikido, Shorinji Kempo, naginata and jukendo are conducted in approximately fifty locations nationwide.
3. International Budo Interaction—International Seminar of Budo Culture for foreign practitioners of budo residing in Japan is conducted annually in March.
4. Kobudo Preservation Activities—Nihon Kobudo Embu Taikai is held annually in February.

Other Activities to Promote Budo and Traditional Culture

1. International Budo Delegations—A delegation made up of representatives from each budo federation is dispatched to a different country each year to perform demonstrations and improve international understanding of the traditional Japanese martial arts.
2. Production of books and monthly journals on budo and calligraphy.
3. Takamadonomiya Cup Nippon Budokan Calligraphy Exhibition—People from all age groups submit works of calligraphy which are displayed at this exhibition held in August. This is the only calligraphy competition in Japan in which the Takamadonomiya Prize is awarded.
4. Library and Museum.
5. Budo Video Library & Archives—A public library containing videos and DVDs relating to modern as well as classical budo.

Nippon Budokan Usage—The facilities at the Nippon Budokan are made available for various budo events such as tournaments and demonstrations. It is also used as a venue for various national, educational, and large-scale commercial events such as concerts etc. The Nippon Budokan also served as the venue for the 1st Kendo World Tokyo Keiko-kai held in June 2012.

The Kendo World (Far Too Brief)
GUIDE to TOKYO

So, you've come to Japan for the World Kendo Championships. Whether you're a competitor or a supporter, chances are you've set aside a day or two to take in the sights. However, this being Tokyo, a city that hosts upwards of 30 million people in the daytime, you may not know where to begin…

Look no further. The staff at Kendo World have collected a premier list of attractions for the 'budo baka'. To begin with, here is a handy English train route and fare calculator: http://www.jorudan.co.jp/english/norikae/

For Culture

THE JAPANESE SWORD MUSEUM

As all kendoka are at heart, and by definition, sword nerds, no trip to New Edo would be complete without a visit to the Japanese Sword Museum. So what if this antique arsenal is somewhat cosier than some might expect and lacking in quality English labels – it's still arguably the greatest public collection of Japanese blades on earth with about 300 swords (not all are on display at once).

The Japanese Sword Museum is about an 8-minute walk from both Sangubashi and Hatsudai stations:
http://www.touken.or.jp/english/

The Japanese Sword Museum

THE IMPERIAL PALACE: MATSU-NO-OROKA

Given the importance of etiquette in kendo, it may also be pertinent to pay a visit to the Imperial Palace in the very heart of Tokyo. On the grounds of the East Gardens is a small stone marking what was once the *matsu-no-oroka* (pine corridor), a grand reception area in long-since-destroyed Edo Castle where the daimyo Asano Takumi-no-Kami Naganori drew a blade on Kira Kozukenosuke Yoshihisa over a point of etiquette, sparking the famous saga of the 47 Ronin. It's just a short walk from the Nippon Budokan.

From Otemachi station (on several subway lines), walk a few minutes to the Otemon gate and enter the palace's East Gardens, which are open to the public.
http://www.japan-guide.com/e/e3018.html

The Imperial Palace with Nijubashi Bridge

MEIJI SHRINE / YOYOGI PARK

Too much time in the concrete jungle can result in a condition known as "Tokyo Panic". If afflicted, a trip to the Meiji Shrine and the neighbouring Yoyogi Park is advised. Nestled in a quiet forest that almost lets you forget you're in a city, this Shinto site is dedicated to Emperor Meiji. Relax and unwind as you follow the gravel path and marvel at the majestic *mon* gates and *sake* offerings. If you're lucky, you may even catch a glimpse of a traditional wedding at the shrine itself. While you're here, take a small detour to Yoyogi Park, just around the corner from the shrine. This is where Tokyoites go to enjoy the outdoors. Running into the sax quartet among the trees is a portent of good luck.

Get off the circular Yamanote line at Harajuku.
http://www.meijijingu.or.jp/english/

The main gate of Meiji Shrine

Meiji Shrine

SENGAKUJI TEMPLE

Speaking of the 47 Ronin, why not make use of your time in Tokyo to pay your respects directly? Sengakuji is by no means a large or majestic temple, yet each year it receives a steady stream of visitors thanks to the presence of the graves of the 47 men whose fealty won them lasting renown. Before being buried alongside their master, the 47 Ronin brought the head of the object of their vengeance here to appease the soul of their lord. At Sengakuji you can burn incense for the famed warriors of old, and learn more about their story at a small museum.

Sengakuji is a short walk from Sengakuji station, or a 15 to 20-minute walk from either Shinagawa or Tamachi stations on the Yamanote Line.
http://www.japan-guide.com/e/e3000.html

Sengakuji Temple

The 47 Ronin Gravesite

OTHER MUSEUMS

For history buffs, the Edo Tokyo Museum (near Ryogoku station) has interactive exhibits and scale models of life in Edo, and the Tokyo National Museum (in Ueno Park) offers a more traditional museum experience with countless historical treasures.

Edo Tokyo Museum

O-EDO ONSEN MONOGATARI

After three days of kendo, whether watching or doing, it's probably high time for a bath. And if you're going to have a bath, are you game enough to do it in the company of strangers? Welcome to *onsen*, perhaps the hottest example of Japanese culture, though it takes some getting used to.

When you enter Oedo Onsen Monogatari, you'll don a *yukata* and step into a self-contained world of small restaurants, bars, and of course luxurious soaking and other spa-related facilities. There really is no better way to unwind.

There are many ways to get here (see the website), but the closest station is Telecom Center station.
http://www.ooedoonsen.jp/en/top/#access

Akihabara Electric Town

AKIHABARA

Anyone with a burning yearning for technology and/or maids will want to put in at Akihabara, a neighbourhood in Tokyo's northeast that is recognised as a tech mecca. Check out the latest in camera and video game gear, or check out one of the famous maid cafes, where (we are told) you can be served by hyper-*kawaii* female staff. We shall leave the internet research up to our dear readers, as there is no shortage of blog entries about this online.

Maids in Akihabara

SHIBUYA

A not-to-be-missed Gordon knot of entertainment, Shibuya is home to the famous "scramble" crossing that sums up Tokyo's bustle so well. A list of recommendations here could go on for pages, but with a little robust exploration, the reader is likely to stumble on some gem that is unknown even to grizzled long-term residents. Start at the Hachiko Exit and don't stop until dawn. Hachiko, by the way, was a small dog.

The world-famous Shibuya Scramble

SHINJUKU

Another major entertainment hub. Be sure to check out "Memory Lane", a.k.a. "Piss Alley", a hive of tiny drinking establishments on a side street by Uniqlo near the station's West Exit. Of equal value is the ever-photogenic "Golden Gai", a grid of themed bars that harkens back to the Tokyo of 60 years ago. Be sure to stop in at Bar Champion, a standing bar with 100-yen-a-song karaoke where Kendo World staff have been known to hone their *kiai* with rousing renditions of The Human League's "Don't You Want Me", or Ian Dury's "Hit Me with Your Rhythm Stick".

Shinjuku

TAKESHITA-DORI

If you want to buy crepes, Hello Kitty merchandise and character goods, or if you are into hip-hop, gothic, metal, emo, maid or schoolgirl fashions, come to Takeshita-dori. If you also suddenly have a hankering to buy a shirt with nonsense English written on it, this is your place!

Extends from Harajuku station on the Yamanote Line.

Takeshita-dori

ORIENTAL BAZAAR

If you want to buy some cheap tat or quality souvenirs to take to your folks back home, look no further than Oriental Bazaar on the main drag in Omotesando.

In between Omotesando, Harajuku and Meiji Jingu-mae stations.
http://www.orientalbazaar.co.jp/en/index.html

Oriental Bazaar

ZANSHIN TOKYO

Call yourself a kendo aficionado? Then, you surely love beer, right? Well, why not combine the two? Take a trip to Zanshin, the kendo themed sports bar. There's even a bogu shop inside!

Near the East Exit of JR Ikebukuro station.
http://www.zanshin.tokyo/in/english/

Zanshin Sports Bar

R. M. Knutsen carrying the British flag at the WGKM. (Courtesy of AJKF)

The Not-So-Well-Known History of International Kendo Competitions

By Michael Ishimatsu-Prime

The history of the World Kendo Championships (WKC) stretches back 45 years. The first WKC was held in 1970 at the Nippon Budokan, and this year, the championships return home in its sixteenth edition. However, there have been a number of international kendo competitions that predate the 1st WKC making a history of 50 years. One such event was the International Goodwill Kendo Club World Championships.

The International Goodwill Kendo Club (IGKC) was formed in September 1965 through the efforts of Wazaki Yoshiyuki, and the purpose of the club was to promote kendo globally. Only two months after its inauguration, the 1st International Goodwill Kendo Club World Championship (IGKCWC) was held in Taipei on 21 November, 1965. Attending this event were 30 competitors from Japan, 11 from Okinawa (which was under U.S.A. administration

at the time), 28 from Chinese Taipei, and four from the U.S.

In November 1966, the 2nd IGKCWC was held in Okinawa at the University of the Ryukyus. This time competitors from Japan, Okinawa, Chinese Taipei and the U.S.A. were also joined by a delegation from Korea.

The 3rd IGKCWC was held in Osaka—the first time on the Japanese mainland—at the Central Gymnasium on 8 October, 1967. Gathered in Osaka were kendoka from Australia (4), Brazil (2), Canada (1), Chinese Taipei (26), France (1), Hawaii (13), Japan (33), Korea (23), Okinawa (15), Switzerland (1), the U.S.A. (18), and W. Germany (1). Korea defeated Japan in the team competition final, and the U.S.A. finished third. The individual competition was won by H. Kumamaru, Chinese

11

Wazaki Yoshiyuki, founder of the IGKC.
(Courtesy of IGKC)

white" match. Held on two *shiai-jō*, there were 41 competitors on each side, who each fought once.

Next there was an *enbu* section. Demonstrating the Nihon Kendo Kata was H10-dan Mochida Moriji as Uchidachi, and H8-dan Torao Mori from the U.S.A. as Shidachi. They were followed by an iai demonstration performed by former Minister of Foreign Affairs, Sonoda Sunao, and then a children's kendo display.

The second half of the *kōhaku-sen* was concluded and was then followed by a naginata display and a *jōjutsu* demonstration by Shimizu Takaji Hanshi and esteemed budo researcher Donn Draeger. Sasamori Junzō (author of *This is Kendo* with Gordon Warner) and Ishida Kazuto then performed some *koryū* kata. Before the team competition started, five *mohan-jiai* matches took place featuring such kendo luminaries as H8-dan Nakakura Kiyoshi and H8-dan Ogasawara Saburō, both of whom were later awarded 9-dan.

The WGKM concluded with the team event in which some of the participating nations competed in two leagues. The A-League was comprised

Taipei's C-T. Wu finished second (he placed third at the 3rd WKC in England, 1976), and a *nitō* kendoka from Japan called Arai took third place.

The number of competitors and countries increased significantly from the 2nd IGKCWC to the third. It is probable that the reason for this is because four days earlier, on 4 October, 1967, another international kendo competition was held— The World Goodwill Kendo Match (WGKM). The World Goodwill Kendo Match represented the first foray by the All Japan Kendo Federation into international competition (the International Kendo Federation had not yet been established), and, like the 1st WKC that was held three years later, it was convened at the Nippon Budokan.

The WGKM was a one-day event and featured competitors from Australia, Brazil, Canada, Chinese Taipei, Great Britain, Hawaii, Japan, Korea, Okinawa, Switzerland, the U.S.A. and W. Germany. Overseeing the tournament as the head *shinpan* was H10-dan Mochida Moriji, and he was no doubt ably supported by court judges Ogawa Chūtarō and Satō Sadao, both H9-dan sensei.

Very different from other kendo competitions, the WGKM started in the late afternoon, at 3.30. Once the opening ceremony and formalities were completed, the first half of the individual competition started. This was not a championship event like the WKC or All Japan Kendo Championships where a winner and runners-up are decided by the end of the day; it was a *kōhaku-sen*—a "red versus

Poster for the 1st IGKCWC. (Courtesy of IGKC)

Participants of the 1st IGKCWC in Taipei.
(Courtesy of IGKC)

Some participants of the 2nd IGKCWC paying a courtesy call
to the U.S.A. High Commission in Okinawa. Gordon Warner is
far right. (Courtesy of IGKC)

Participants of the 2nd IGKCWC in an open-car parade
down International Street in Okinawa. (Courtesy of IGKC)

Competitors at the 2nd IGKCWC in Okinawa.
(Courtesy of IGKC)

The Nihon Kendo Kata being performed by H8-dan Torao
Mori (L) and H10-dan Mochida Moriji (R) at the WGKM.
(Courtesy of AJKF)

Gordon Warner at the WGKM. (Courtesy of AJKF)

Jōjutsu enbu by Shimizu Takaji Hanshi and Donn Draeger
at the WGKM. (Courtesy of AJKF)

The teams at the WGKM Opening Ceremony. (Courtesy of AJKF)

The WGKM Opening Ceremony. (Courtesy of AJKF)

Chinese Taipei competitor in the team competition at the WGKM. (Courtesy of AJKF)

The mixed team at the WGKM. (Courtesy of AJKF)

The victorious Japanese team at the closing ceremony of the WGKM. (Courtesy of AJKF)

Chinese Taipei receiving the WGKM runners up trophy.
(Courtesy of AJKF)

The Korea and Okinawa teams receiving an award at the WGKM.
(Courtesy of AJKF)

of Japan, Korea, and Hawaii; the B-League was contested by Chinese Taipei, the U.S.A., Okinawa and a mixed team of different nationalities. There are no surviving records of the league match results, but Japan and Chinese Taipei must have won their respective leagues as the former beat the latter 4-1 in the final.

According to Shōji Munemitsu's *Kendo hyakunen* (100 Years of Kendo), the AJKF decided to organise the WGKM because the number of countries interested in Japanese kendo was increasing, totalling over ten at that time. Its purpose was to strengthen the bonds of friendship between practitioners of different countries and to contribute to the spread of kendo throughout the world.

An article in the 4th WKC program states that at a meeting following the WGKM, Torao Mori-sensei "strongly requested" to the representatives of the 11 participating countries that an international kendo organisation be formed. Consensus was reached between all of the participating nations, and they decided that the IKF (later changed to FIK) would be formed. The AJKF decided to organise the 1st WKC to be held in 1970. The IKF was officially inaugurated on April 4, 1970, the day before the team event of the 1st WKC. The individual event was convened in Osaka on April 10. Mori-sensei did not get to see the WKC for himself as he tragically passed away from a heart attack in January 1969.

The formation of the IKF did not end the activities of the IGKC. It is still going strong and was awarded the status of a Non-Profit Organisation by the Japanese government in 1999. The IGKC regularly holds meetings in various regions around Japan, in addition to conducting overseas seminars. Its yearly meeting in November attracts participants from Chinese Taipei, Korea, Hong Kong and even further afield.

The number of participating federations increased from 11 at the WGKM to 17 at the 1st WKC. At the 16th WKC, 50 years since the WGKM, the Nippon Budokan will welcome competitors and officials from 56 federations—a five-fold increase from 1967—demonstrating the continued spread and popularisation of kendo throughout the world. The future is bright for kendo.

History of the WKC

Compiled by Alex Bennett and Michael Ishimatsu-Prime

1st World Kendo Championships

Location: Tokyo (Team)–Osaka (Individual), Japan

Venue: Nippon Budokan (Team), Osaka Central Gymnasium (Individual)

Date: April 5, 1970 (Team); April 10, 1970 (Individual)

Participating Federations: (17) Australia, Belgium, Brazil, Canada, Chinese Taipei, France, Great Britain, Hawaii, Japan, Korea, Morocco, Netherlands, New Zealand, Okinawa, Switzerland, U.S.A.

Results:

Men's Team:

1st	Japan
2nd	Chinese Taipei
3rd	Brazil / Okinawa

Men's Individual:

1st	M. Kobayashi (JPN)
2nd	T. Toda (JPN)
3rd	Y. Taniguchi (JPN)
	T. Ōta (JPN)

Trivia:

- The International Kendo Federation was launched on April 4 at the Nippon Budokan.
- The venues for the team and individual events were split between Tokyo and Osaka respectively.
- Of the 17 federations that participated, 11 took part in the team event.
- 128 competitors entered the individual event.
- Four women also competed.
- As Okinawa was under American administration at the time, it made an appearance as a separate federation. Control of Okinawa was handed back to Japan in 1972, so this was the first and last time.
- Well-known *nitō* kendoka, H8-dan Toda Tadao-sensei, was at the time a 30-year-old R5-dan *jōdan* competitor. He was defeated in the final by a *tsuki*.
- 49-year-old K7-dan Taniguchi Yasunori, who finished 3rd, would eventually become a H9-dan. He is the master in the famous video taking on much younger sensei during the interval of the AJKF's 50th anniversary.
- There were 96 competitors in the *kōhaku-sen* (red vs. white) competition.
- World-famous novelist Mishima Yukio participated in the *kōhaku-sen*. He was 5-dan at the time. A little over six months later, Mishima committed *seppuku* in the offices of the Japan Self-Defence Forces after attempting to stage a coup d'état to restore power to the emperor.
- Linesmen were used in the matches to identify if competitors stepped out.
- The crown prince and his wife, Michiko-sama, attended some of the matches.
- An international kendo demonstration was also held at the Osaka Expo being held at the time.

Men's Team Best-4

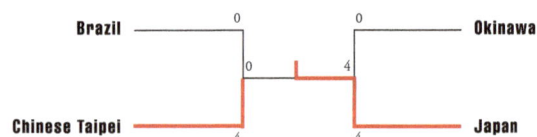

Key

M = *men*, K = *kote*, D = *dō*, T = *tsuki*

本 = win by no. of *ippon* scored

代 = win by *daihyō-sen*

Men's Individual Best-16

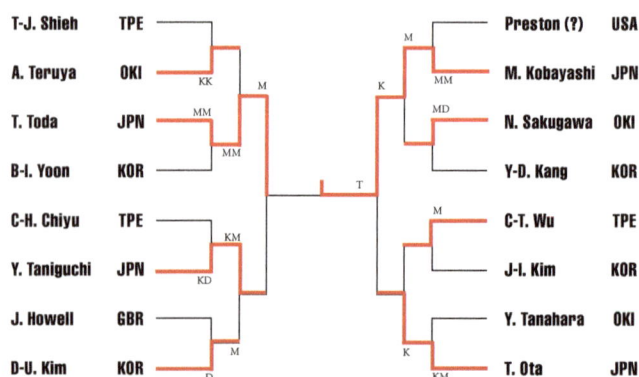

The first International Kendo Federation meeting held on April 4, 1970, held at the Hilton Hotel. (Courtesy of AJKF)

Representatives of each national team being presented with souvenirs at the welcome party. (Courtesy of AJKF)

1st WKC welcome party. (Courtesy of AJKF)

The Nippon Budokan in 1970. (Courtesy of AJKF)

President of the AJKF, Kimura Tokutarō, making a welcome speech at the Nippon Budokan. (Courtesy of AJKF)

Opening ceremony. (Courtesy of AJKF)

Competitors' oath being made by Sakakibara of Japan. (Courtesy of AJKF)

Koryū demonstration. (Courtesy of AJKF)

Children's training demonstration. (Courtesy of AJKF)

President of the AJKF, Kimura Tokutarō (R) with other dignitaries and the trophies. (Courtesy of AJKF)

Team competition matches. Notice the linesmen at the edge of the courts. (Courtesy of AJKF)

A Chinese Taipei competitor fighting a Japanese kendoka with the Crown Prince and Michiko-sama watching. (Courtesy of AJKF)

Great Britain's John Howell preparing for his match. (Courtesy of AJKF)

Japanese team being presented with their winner's medals. (Courtesy of AJKF)

Closing ceremony. (Courtesy of AJKF)

Competitors and officials on the bullet train from Tokyo to Nagoya on April 6, 1970, the day after the team event at the Nippon Budokan. (Courtesy of AJKF)

The World Kendo Nagoya Match held on April 6, 1970, at Meiji-mura. (Courtesy of AJKF)

Nihon Kendo Kata demonstration at the World Kendo Nagoya Match held on April 6, 1970, at Meiji-mura. (Courtesy of AJKF)

Osaka World Expo, 1970. (Courtesy of AJKF)

Iaido demonstration at the Osaka World Expo. (Courtesy of AJKF)

Kendo demonstration at the Osaka World Expo. (Courtesy of AJKF)

Opening ceremony of the 1st WKC Individual Competition at Osaka City Central Gymnasium on April 10, 1970. (Courtesy of AJKF)

Opening ceremony of the 1st WKC Individual Competition at Osaka City Central Gymnasium on April 10, 1970. (Courtesy of AJKF)

Opening speech at the 1st WKC individual competition. (Courtesy of AJKF)

Nihon Kendo Kata demonstration at the 1st WKC Individual Competition. (Courtesy of AJKF)

1st WKC individual match. (Courtesy of AJKF)

1st WKC individual match. (Courtesy of AJKF)

Kobayashi Mitsuru receiving his Individual Competition winner's medal. (Courtesy of AJKF)

Chinese Taipei's T-J. Shieh being awarded with a Fighting Spirit award. (Courtesy of AJKF)

19

2nd World Kendo Championships

Location: Los Angeles (Team)–San Francisco (Individual), U.S.A.

Venue: Los Angeles Memorial Sports Arena (Team), San Francisco Winterland (Individual)

Date: April 8, 1973 (Team); April 15, 1973 (Individual)

Participating Federations: (16) Australia, Brazil, Canada, China, France, Great Britain, Hawaii, Hong Kong, Japan, Korea, Malaysia, Morocco, Portugal, Sweden, Switzerland, U.S.A.

Results:

Men's Team:
1st	Japan
2nd	Canada
3rd	U.S.A. / Hawaii

Men's Individual:
1st	T. Sakuragi (JPN)
2nd	H. Yano (JPN)
3rd	T. Fujita (JPN)
	J-R. Rhee (KOR)

Debut Federations:
Hong Kong, Malaysia, Portugal

Trivia:
- Despite three countries making their debut, the number of participating federations decreased by one from the previous tournament.
- Only eight teams—Brazil, Canada, Chinese Taipei, France, Hawaii, Japan, Korea and U.S.A.—participated in the team event.
- Two four-team leagues were formed: Group A and Group B. The top two of each league progressed to the semi-final.
- The league results were: Group A—1st, Japan; 2nd, Canada; 3rd, Korea; 4th, Brazil. Group B—1st, U.S.A.; 2nd, Hawaii; 3rd, France; 4th, Chinese Taipei.
- This is the only time all three North American federations finished in the medal positions.
- 58 competitors competed in the individual competition. Seven out of eight quarter-finalists were Japanese.
- Japan's Kantoku was the legendary Nakakura Kiyoshi-sensei.
- A goodwill tournament was also held in San Jose at California State University on April 13, 1973.
- *Ishu-jiai* matches against naginata also featured at the tournament.

The third-place U.S.A. team. (Courtesy of Jeff Marsten)

Men's Team Best-4

Japan — 5
Hawaii — 0
4
Japan — 1
Canada — 2
U.S.A. — 1 / 0

Men's Individual Best-16

H-S. Chang	TPE	MM	
H. Yano	JPN	MM MD	
F. Iwaya	JPN		
P. Toida	BRA		
A. Fukutomi	HWI		
M. Kojima	JPN	K	
T. Fujita	JPN	M	
N. Yoshida	BRA	M	

M. Kurihara	JPN	KD M	
M. Yamaguchi	USA		
J-R. Rhee	KOR	MM KK	
K. Hao	CAN		
T. Nakamura	JPN	K D	
H-M. Do	KOR		
J-P. Reniez	FRA	MM MK	
T. Sakuragi	JPN	KK	

MM (center)

3rd World Kendo Championships

Location: Milton Keynes, England

Venue: Bletchley Leisure Centre

Date: April 17–18, 1976

Participating Federations: (20) Australia, Belgium, Brazil, Canada, China, France, Great Britain, Hawaii, Hong Kong, Italy, Japan, Korea, Malaysia, Morocco, Netherlands, Singapore, Sweden, Switzerland, U.S.A., W. Germany

Results:

Men's Team:
- 1st Japan
- 2nd Canada
- 3rd U.S.A. / Chinese Taipei

Men's Individual:
- 1st E. Yokoo (JPN)
- 2nd K. Ono (JPN)
- 3rd I. Hosoda (JPN)
-       C-T. Wu (TPE)

Debut Federations: Germany, Italy, Singapore

Trivia:
- 200 competitors were present, with 105 of them fighting in the individuals.
- 17 teams competed in the team event, but Korea was not present.
- Japan won the quarter-final, semi-final and final rounds 5–0, against France, the U.S.A. and Canada respectively.
- For the second tournament running, seven of the eight quarter-finalists in the individual tournament were Japanese.
- There were goodwill matches with competitors from Austria, Belgium, France, Great Britain, Hawaii, Netherlands, Sweden, Switzerland, U.S.A., W. Germany.
- Satō Nariaki-sensei of the University of Tsukuba also competed for the Japanese team.

THE INTERNATIONAL KENDO FEDERATION

3rd. World Kendo Championship ENGLAND 1976

Organised by: The British Kendo Association

J. Clerc (L) of Switzerland versus Great Britain's Tony Palmer. (Courtesy of the Holt family)

The Great Britain team. (Courtesy of the Holt family)

A kendo themed Toby jug made by Deborah Hopson for the 3rd WKC. (Courtesy of the Holt family)

Men's Team Best-8

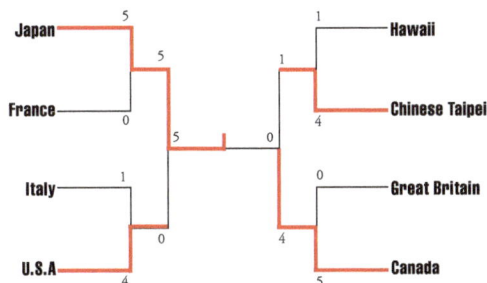

Men's Individual Best-16

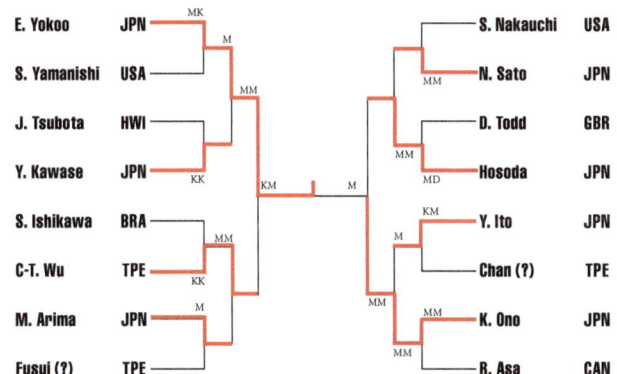

4th World Kendo Championships

Location: Sapporo, Japan

Venue: Makomanai Ice Arena

Date: August 4–5, 1979

Participating Federations: (21) Argentina, Australia, Austria, Belgium, Brazil, Canada, France, Great Britain, Hawaii, Hong Kong, Italy, Japan, Korea, Malaysia, Netherlands, Portugal, Spain, Sweden, Switzerland, U.S.A., W. Germany

Results:

Men's Team:
	1st	Japan
	2nd	Korea
	3rd	U.S.A. / Hawaii

Men's Individual:
	1st	H. Yamada (JPN)
	2nd	K. Furukawa (JPN)
	3rd	K. Terada (JPN)
		H. Aikawa (JPN)

Debut Federations: Argentina, Austria, Spain

Trivia:
- 21 of the 25 affiliated federations participated, with only Chinese Taipei, Singapore, New Zealand and Morocco not taking part.
- 126 competitors fought in the individuals. Five Japanese, two Korean, and one American made it to the quarter-finals.
- 18 countries competed in the team competition.
- Japan won their first two matches 5-0, but Great Britain's Mike Davis fighting as Taishō defeated I. Ogawa with a *dō* and *men* strike to finish the match 4-1. Mike Davis was awarded a fighting spirit award.
- Mike Davis was also chosen to compete in the *mohan-jiai* (demonstration matches) section.
- This was Korea's first time to reach the final.
- 15 of the 25 *shinpan* were non-Japanese.

Great Britain's Mike Davis (R) beating Japans' Ogawa in the Taishō round of the team competition with a *men* and *dō* strike. (Courtesy of AJKF)

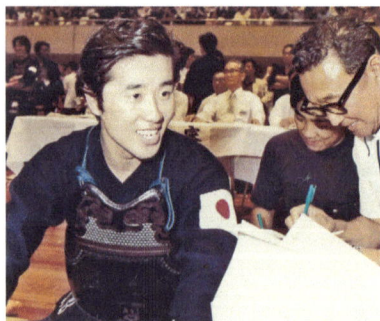

Individual competition runner-up and future 8-dan champion Furukawa Kazuo talking to the press. (Courtesy of AJKF)

Furukawa Kazuo's runner-up trophy. (Courtesy of AJKF)

Individual winner Yamada receiving his trophy. (Courtesy of AJKF)

The Great Britain team getting ready. (Courtesy of AJKF)

The victorious Japanese team. (Courtesy of AJKF)

Men's Team Best-8

Japan	4		4	Korea
Great Britain	1	3	5	Brazil
		4	1	
U.S.A.	5	0	2	Hawaii
Sweden	0	2	0	Canada
			1	

Men's Individual Best-16

Left side:
- K-Y. Suh — KOR
- H. Yamada — JPN (KT, M, MM)
- M. Fujii — JPN (M)
- J-I. Kim — KOR (MM)
- G. Palomino — SPA
- T. Suzuki — JPN (MM)
- T-K. Kim — KOR
- H. Aikawa — JPN (DM, MD)

Center: KM, KK, D, MD, MK, K, M

Right side:
- J-P. Raick — FRA
- S. Nakauchi — USA
- T. Kurasawa — USA
- K. Furukawa — JPN (MM, M)
- K-C. Ko — KOR (MK)
- H. Ohno — JPN
- R. Someya — BRA
- K. Terada — JPN (MM)

5th World Kendo Championships

Location: São Paulo, Brazil

Venue: Ginásio do Ibirapeura

Date: July 29–August 3, 1982

Participating Federations: (20) Argentina, Australia, Brazil, Canada, Chinese Taipei, France, Great Britain, Hawaii, Italy, Japan, Malaysia, Mexico, Poland, Portugal, Korea, Spain, Sweden, Switzerland, U.S.A., W. Germany

Number of Competitors: 200

Results

Men's Team:
- 1st Japan
- 2nd Brazil
- 3rd Korea / Canada

Men's Individual:
- 1st M. Makita (JPN)
- 2nd T. Kosaka (JPN)
- 3rd T. Okajima (JPN)
-      H. Yasugahira (JPN)

Debut Federations:
Mexico, Poland

Trivia:
- Each country was limited to seven competitors for the individual tournament. 96 were entered.
- The Japanese team arrival was delayed due to a plane accident in New York. They arrived the night before the competition.
- Three Japanese competitors were knocked out in the first and second rounds.
- The remaining four proceeded to the semi-finals.
- Makita Minoru, winner of the individual tournament, was recruited as a teacher for the newly created International Budo University. He retired in 2015 as the president of the university.
- There were 14 teams in the team competition.
- Brazil defeated Korea in the team semi-final through *daihyō-sen*.

FEDERAÇÃO INTERNACIONAL DE KENDO
5: CAMPEONATO MUNDIAL DE KENDO
DIAS: 29 DE JULHO A 03 DE AGOSTO DE 1982
LOCAL: GINÁSIO POLIESPORTIVO "CONSTANCIO VAZ GUIMARÃES" DO IBIRAPUERA
SÃO PAULO-BRASIL

Men's Team Best-8

Japan	5		2	Hawaii
W. Germany	0	5	2代	
		4	1	Brazil
Chinese Taipei	2	0	3	
U.S.A.	3	0	0	France
			2	Korea
			5	

Men's Individual Best-16

Left side:
- G. Nakatani — USA
- J-W. Lee — KOR (KK)
- M. Makita — JPN (D)
- C-B. Lee — KOR (K)
- R. Kaneshiro — USA (KM)
- Y. Nakada — JPN
- T. Okajima — JPN (MM)
- C-P. Hsu — TPE (DM)

Center: DM, MK, MK, M, D, KK

Right side:
- H-G. Jang — KOR (MK)
- D. Johnson — CAN
- H. Yasugahira — JPN (KM, M, D)
- H-H. Kang — KOR
- M. Grivas — USA (KM)
- W-L. Lee — TPE
- T. Kosaka — JPN (KD)
- K-C. Ko — KOR

23

6th World Kendo Championships

Location: Paris, France

Venue: Stade Pierre-de-Coubertin

Date: April 13-14, 1985

Participating Federations:
(25) Argentina, Australia, Austria, Belgium, Brazil, Canada, Chinese Taipei, France, Great Britain, Hawaii, Hong Kong, Italy, Japan, Korea, Malaysia, Mexico, Netherlands, New Zealand, Poland, Portugal, Spain, Sweden, Switzerland, U.S.A., W. Germany

Results:

Men's Team:
1st	Japan	
2nd	Brazil	
3rd	Korea / Canada	

Men's Individual:
1st	K. Kōda (JPN)	
2nd	H. Ogawa (JPN)	
3rd	J-C. Park (KOR)	
	K-N. Kim (KOR)	

Trivia:
- No federations made their debut in this WKC.
- 23 countries were represented in the team event.
- 145 competitors fought in the individual event.
- Female kendoka Sue Lytollis represented New Zealand in the men's team competition.
- Two Japanese were knocked out in the first round. The remaining five proceeded to the quarter-finals, along with three Koreans.
- The two Koreans that shared third place were university students.

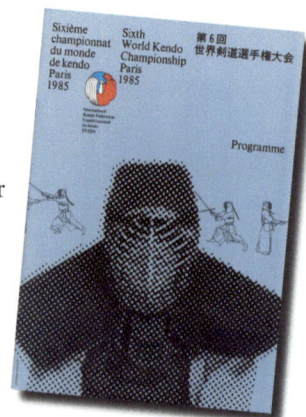

Photos for the 6th~12 WKC courtesy of *Kendo Nihon*

Y-C. Park (Korea) scores *kote* immediately after conceding a *kote* to Gerard Paglieri (France) in the second-round of the team competition.

Kōda Kunihide scores *kote* against Ogawa Haruki in the final of the men's individual competition.

Men's Team Best-14

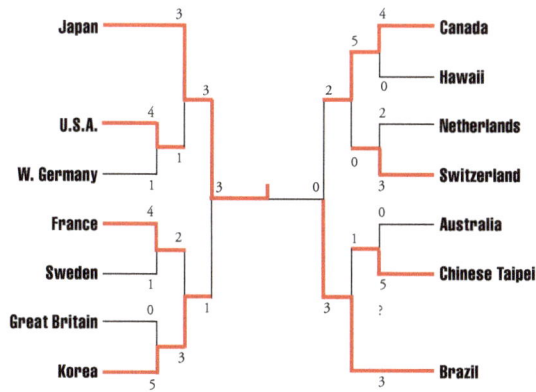

Japan — 3
U.S.A. — 4
W. Germany — 1
France — 4
Sweden — 1
Great Britain — 0
Korea — 5

Canada — 4
Hawaii — 0
Netherlands — 2
Switzerland — 3
Australia — 0
Chinese Taipei — 5
Brazil — 3

(Bracket scores: 3, 3, 1, 2, 1, 3, 0, 3, 5, 2, 0, 0, 3, ?, 3)

Men's Individual Best-16

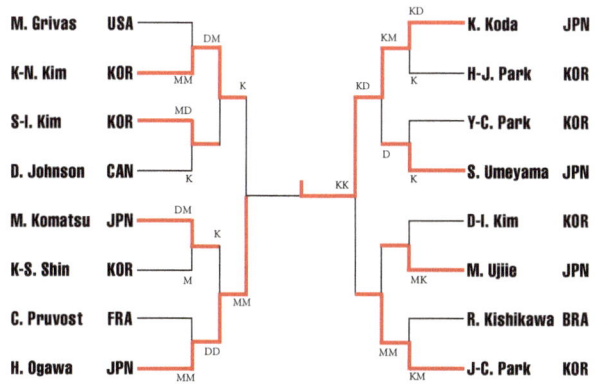

M. Grivas — USA
K-N. Kim — KOR
S-I. Kim — KOR
D. Johnson — CAN
M. Komatsu — JPN
K-S. Shin — KOR
C. Pruvost — FRA
H. Ogawa — JPN

K. Koda — JPN
H-J. Park — KOR
Y-C. Park — KOR
S. Umeyama — JPN
D-I. Kim — KOR
M. Ujiie — JPN
R. Kishikawa — BRA
J-C. Park — KOR

(Bracket notations: DM, MM, MD, K, K, DM, M, MM, DD, MM, KD, KM, K, D, K, MK, MM, KM, KD, KK)

7th World Kendo Championships

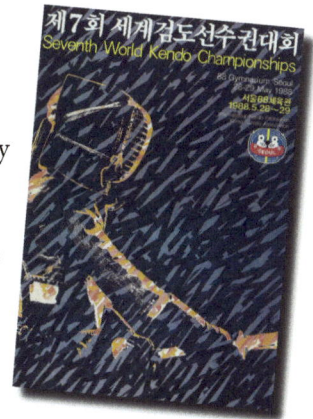

Location: Seoul, South Korea

Venue: 88 Sports Centre

Date: May 28–29, 1988

Participating Federations:
(23) Argentina, Australia, Austria, Belgium, Brazil, Canada, Chinese Taipei, France, Great Britain, Hawaii, Hong Kong, Japan, Korea, Malaysia, Mexico, Netherlands, New Zealand, Norway, Spain, Sweden, Switzerland, U.S.A., W. Germany

Results:

Men's Team:
- 1st Japan
- 2nd Korea
- 3rd Brazil / Canada

Men's Individual:
- 1st I. Okido (JPN)
- 2nd A. Hayashi (JPN)
- 3rd H. Sakata (JPN)
- K-N. Kim (KOR)

Debut Federations: Norway

Trivia:
- This was the year of the Seoul Olympics.
- Ten of Japan's 12 representatives were police.
- 21 countries competed in the team event.
- Nishikawa Kiyoshi, Japan's Fukushō, scored two *katate-tsuki* in the final against Korea. Japan won the match by 1 point, the closest final to date.
- Hayashi Akira of Japan defeated K-N. Kim of Korea by two *kote* in the semi-final match. Kim was clearly unhappy with the *shinpan* decisions, as were the Korean supporters.
- Drink cans and cups were hurled onto the court from the stands, and mayhem looked set to break out for 15 minutes.
- The WKC has not been held in Korea since. The 17th WKC, however, will be held in Korea in 2018.

In the Chūken match of the team final, Miyazaki Masahiro scores *men* against Korea's K-S. Sin.

Japan's Iwahori Tōru was trailing K-N. Kim after conceding a *kote* strike. He rushed in to attempt *dō* but Kim leaped backwards and struck *men* to win the Taishō match of the team final.

Brazil's Roberto Kishikawa scores *dō* against Korea's K-S. Sin.

K-N. Kim looks dismayed after losing his semi-final individual match against Japan's Hayashi Akira.

Men's Team Best-14

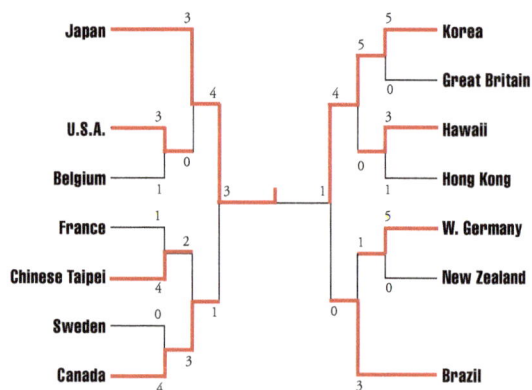

Men's Individual Best-16

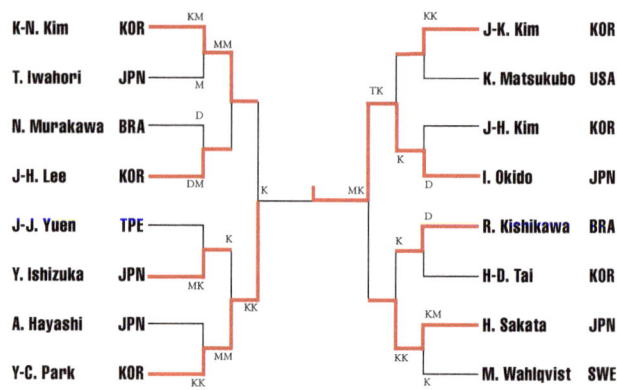

8th World Kendo Championships

Location: Toronto, Canada

Venue: Varsity Arena

Date: June 29–30, 1991

Participating Federations:
(29) Argentina, Australia, Belgium, Brazil, Canada, Chinese Taipei, Denmark, Finland, France, Germany, Great Britain, Hawaii, Hong Kong, Hungary, Italy, Japan, Korea, Malaysia, Mexico, Netherlands, New Zealand, Norway, Poland, Portugal, Singapore, Spain, Sweden, Switzerland, U.S.A.

Results:

Men's Team:	1st	Japan
	2nd	Korea
	3rd	Canada / Chinese Taipei

Men's Individual:	1st	S. Mutō (JPN)
	2nd	H. Sakata (JPN)
	3rd	M. Yamamoto (JPN)
		S. Shimizu (JPN)

Debut Federations:
Denmark, Finland, Hungary

Trivia:
- 29 countries participated in the team event.
- In the tournament stage of the team competition, Japan won all their matches 5–0.
- Chinese Taipei defeated Brazil in the quarter-finals to place third for the first time since the 3WKC.
- Canada defeated the U.S.A. in the quarter-finals to place for the third consecutive time.
- 165 competitors registered for the individual event.
- All four semi-finalists in the individual event were Japanese for the first time in three tournaments.
- Exhibition matches of women and children were held.

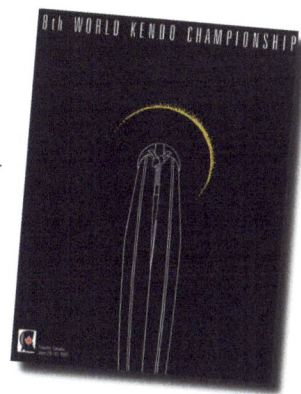

The victorious Japanese men's team wave to the crowd after collecting the championship trophy.

The U.S.A.'s Jason Yamamoto scores *kote* against France's Claude Pruvost in the second-round of the team competition.

The Canadian team celebrate after beating the U.S.A. 3-2 in the quarter-final.

Men's Team Best-16

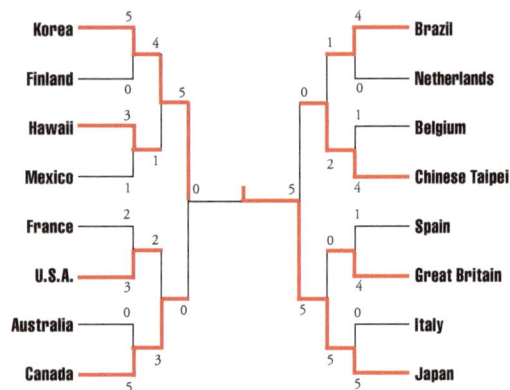

```
Korea     5
            4
Finland   0
              5
Hawaii    3
            1
Mexico    1
                0
France    2
            2
U.S.A.    3
              0
Australia 0
            0
Canada    5
            3
                    5
Brazil        4
                1
Netherlands   0
                  0
Belgium       1
                2
Chinese Taipei 4
                    5
Spain         1
                0
Great Britain 4
                  5
Italy         0
                5
Japan         5
```

Men's Individual Best-16

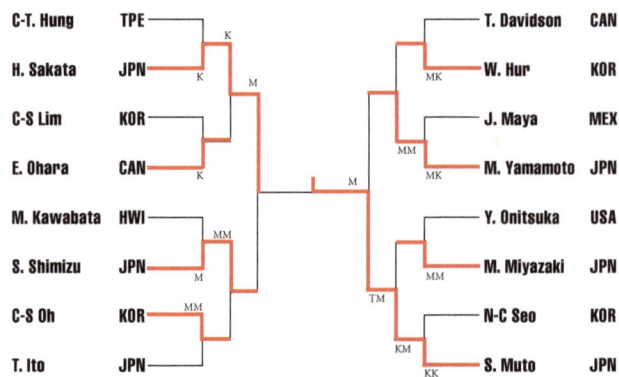

```
C-T. Hung   TPE
                 K
H. Sakata   JPN      K
                        M
C-S Lim     KOR
                 K
E. Ohara    CAN
                            M
M. Kawabata HWI
                     MM
S. Shimizu  JPN  M
                        MM
C-S Oh      KOR  MM
T. Ito      JPN
                                TM
T. Davidson CAN
                     MK
W. Hur      KOR          MK
J. Maya     MEX      MM
M. Yamamoto JPN  MK
                            M
Y. Onitsuka USA
                     MM
M. Miyazaki JPN  MM
N-C Seo     KOR          KM
S. Muto     JPN  KK
```

9th World Kendo Championships

Location: Paris, France

Venue: Stade Pierre-de-Coubertin

Date: April 8–10, 1994

Participating Federations:
(32) Argentina, Australia, Austria, Belgium, Brazil, Canada, Chinese Taipei, Czech Republic, Finland, France, Germany, Great Britain, Hawaii, Hong Kong, Hungary, Iceland, Italy, Japan, Korea, Malaysia, Mexico, Netherlands, New Zealand, Norway, Poland, Singapore, South Africa, Spain, Sweden, Switzerland, U.S.A., Yugoslavia

Results:

Men's Team:		
	1st	Japan
	2nd	Korea
	3rd	Chinese Taipei
		Canada

Men's Individual:		
	1st	H. Takahashi (JPN)
	2nd	K. Takei (JPN)
	3rd	S. Hirano (JPN)
		N. Eiga (JPN)

Debut Federations: Czech Republic, Iceland, South Africa, Yugoslavia

Trivia:
- The 9WKC were conducted at the same venue as the 6WKC.
- The Goodwill Tournament featured Junior Boys, Women's Team, Women's Individual, Men's 4-dan and below, Men's 5-dan and above competitions.
- A 15-member Japanese women's team took on a combined men's and women's team from Europe and won 12-1 (2 draws).
- 32 teams competed in the team event making it the biggest tournament to date.
- Teams were divided into ten blocks and the top two teams in each block proceeded to the knockout tournament.
- For the second tournament running, the top four results in the men's team competition were the same.
- For the third consecutive tournament, Japan and Korea meet in the finals. Japan defeated Korea 4-0, but most agreed that the match was much closer than the score indicated.

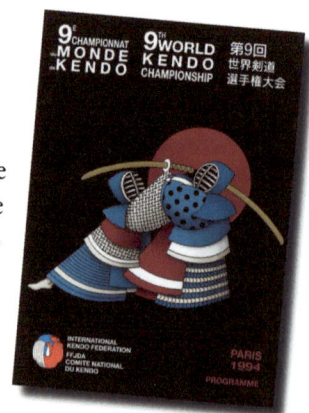

Takahashi goes for *men* against Takei in the all-Japan men's individual final.

In the team final Jihō match, Miyazaki evades K-M. Jeong's *katate-men* strike.

In the quarter-final team match, Canada's Matthew Raymond attempts to strike Ishida Toshiya's *kote*.

Men's Team Best-16

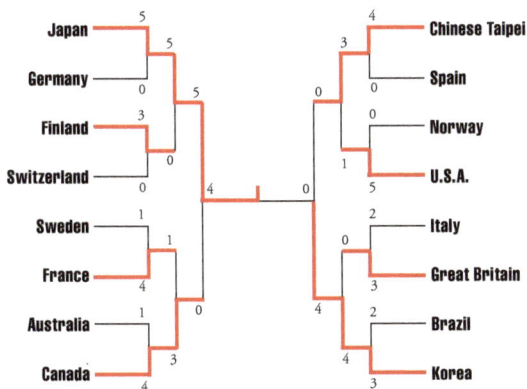

Men's Individual Best-16

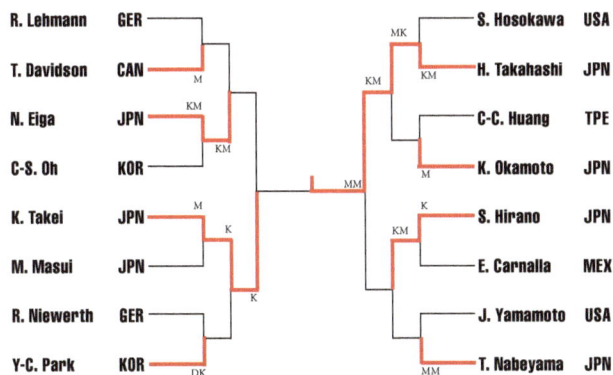

10th World Kendo Championships

Location: Kyoto, Japan

Venue: Kyoto City Gymnasium

Date: September 27–30,

Participating Federations:
(34) Argentina, Australia, Austria, Belgium, Brazil, Canada, Chinese Taipei, Denmark, Finland, France, Germany, Great Britain, Hawaii, Hong Kong, Hungary, Iceland, Italy, Japan, Korea, Luxembourg, Malaysia, Netherlands, New Zealand, Norway, Poland, Romania, Singapore, South Africa, Spain, Sweden, Switzerland, U.S.A., Venezuela, Yugoslavia

Results:

Men's Team I:
1st Japan
2nd Korea
3rd Brazil
Chinese Taipei

Men's Team II:
1st Hungary
2nd Sweden
3rd Italy / Romania

Men's Individual:
1st M. Miyazaki (JPN)
2nd F. Miyazaki (JPN)
3rd T. Ishida (JPN)
S-S. Park (KOR)

Women's Invitational Team:

1st	Japan B
2nd	Japan A
3rd	U.S.A. B
	Korea A

Women's Individual (3-dan~):

1st	M. Kimura (JPN)
2nd	S. Mogi (JPN)
3rd	W. Nakano (CAN)
	H-J. Cho (KOR)

Women's Individual (~2-dan):

1st	S. Takashima (JPN)
2nd	M. Onaka (BRA)
3rd	E-J. Lee (KOR)
	J-Y. Kwon (KOR)

Debut Federations: Luxembourg, Romania, Venezuela

Trivia:

- Group I was made up of four groups of three teams. The top two in each went through to the tournament stage.
- In Group II, all of the semi-finalists were European teams.
- Each country was limited to five entries only for the individual competition.
- Jean-Pierre Labru (France) was the first European to make the best-8 of the men's individual competition.
- The Miyazaki brothers from the Kanagawa Police met in the final. Older brother, Masahiro, won the match to add the world title to his collection of four national titles.
- Younger brother, Fumihiro, avenged his loss and defeated his brother to win the national championship for the first and only time later this year.

The opening ceremony.

Iaido *enbu* in the grounds of Heian Shrine a few days before the start of the WKC.

H-T. Lin of Chinese Taipei scores a *kote* against Spain's David Castro in the Chūken match of the quarter-final.

In the Senpō match of the 2nd Division final, Hungary's Tibor Barany scores *men* against his Swedish opponent.

In the men's individual competition, S-S. Park of Korea scores the first of two *kote* against France's J-P. Labru.

Hawaii's Henry Smalls scores a *debana-men*.

Men's Team I Best-8

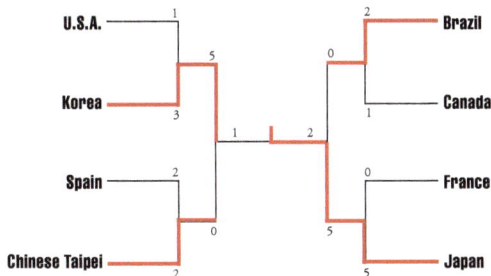

U.S.A.	1	2 Brazil
	5	0 Canada 1
Korea	3	
	1	2
Spain	2	0 France
	0	5
Chinese Taipei	2	5 Japan

Men's Team II Best-14

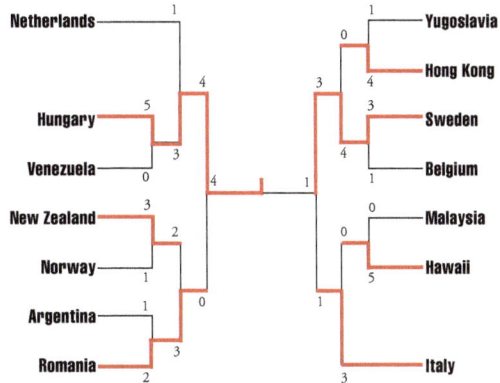

Netherlands	1	1 Yugoslavia
	4	0
Hungary	5	3 Hong Kong
	3	4 3 Sweden
Venezuela	0	4 4 Belgium 1
	4	1
New Zealand	3	0 Malaysia
Norway	2 / 1	0 5 Hawaii
	0	1
Argentina	1	
Romania	3 / 2	3 Italy

Women's Invitational Team Best-16

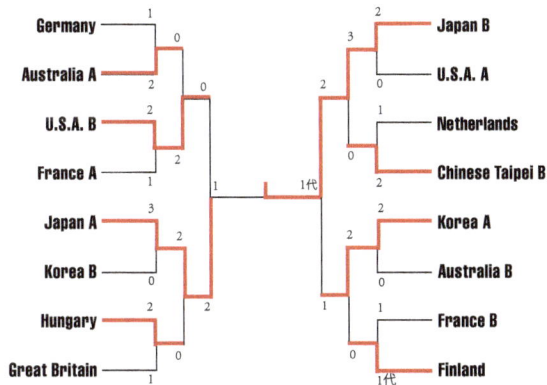

Germany	1	2 Japan B
	0	3
Australia A	2	2 U.S.A. A
	0	
U.S.A. B	2	2 1 Netherlands
France A	2 / 1	0
	1	2 Chinese Taipei B
Japan A	3	1fL
	2	2 Korea A
Korea B	0	2
	2	1 Australia B
Hungary	2	1 France B
Great Britain	0 / 1	0
		1fL Finland

Men's Individual Best-16

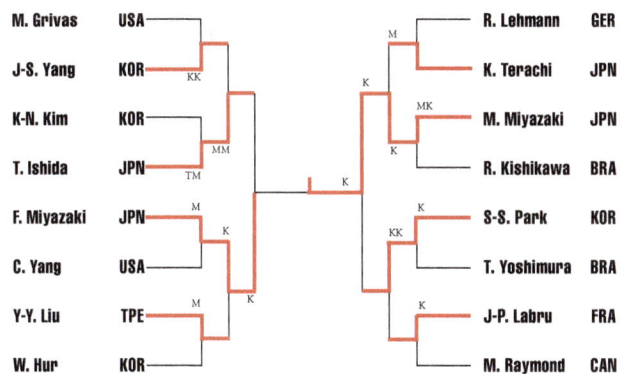

M. Grivas	USA		R. Lehmann	GER
	KK	M		
J-S. Yang	KOR		K. Terachi	JPN
	MM	K		
K-N. Kim	KOR		M. Miyazaki	JPN
	TM	MK		
T. Ishida	JPN	K	R. Kishikawa	BRA
		K		
F. Miyazaki	JPN	M	S-S. Park	KOR
	K	KK		
C. Yang	USA	K	T. Yoshimura	BRA
	M	K		
Y-Y. Liu	TPE	K	J-P. Labru	FRA
W. Hur	KOR		M. Raymond	CAN

Women's Individual (3-dan~) Best-16

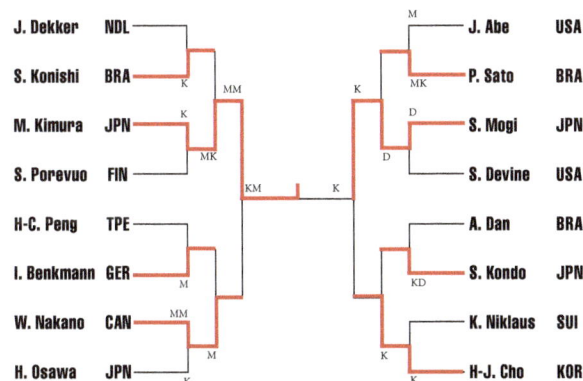

J. Dekker	NDL	M	J. Abe	USA
	K	MK		
S. Konishi	BRA	MM	P. Sato	BRA
M. Kimura	JPN	K	D	S. Mogi	JPN
	MK	D		
S. Porevuo	FIN	KM	K	S. Devine	USA
H-C. Peng	TPE		A. Dan	BRA
	M	KD		
I. Benkmann	GER		S. Kondo	JPN
W. Nakano	CAN	MM	K	K. Niklaus	SUI
	M	K		
H. Osawa	JPN	K	H-J. Cho	KOR

Women's Individual (~2-dan) Best-16

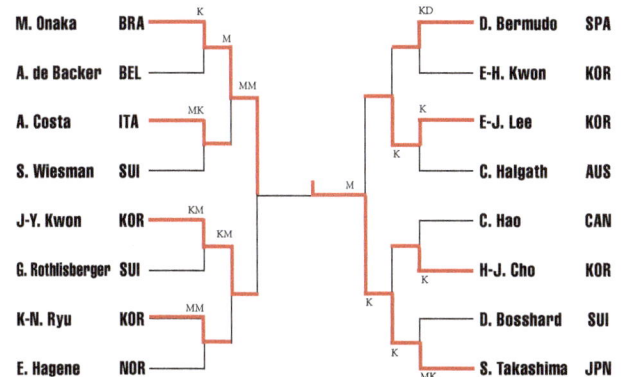

M. Onaka	BRA	K	KD	D. Bermudo	SPA
	M			
A. de Backer	BEL	MM	E-H. Kwon	KOR
A. Costa	ITA	MK	K	E-J. Lee	KOR
		K		
S. Wiesman	SUI	M	C. Halgath	AUS
J-Y. Kwon	KOR	KM	C. Hao	CAN
	KM	K		
G. Rothlisberger	SUI		H-J. Cho	KOR
K-N. Ryu	KOR	MM	K	D. Bosshard	SUI
	K	MK		
E. Hagene	NOR		S. Takashima	JPN

Reviewing the History and Challenges of Women's Participation at the WKC

By Kate Sylvester

The 1st World Kendo Championship was held in Tokyo in 1970. Fifteen years later at the 6th WKC held in France, 26-year-old 2-dan Sue Lytollis of New Zealand was selected to fight in the men's team event. In the team competition, Lytollis recalls scoring an *ippon* against her Hawaiian opponent which earned her a roar of cheers from the spectators. At the 7th WKC held in Korea three years later in 1988, Lytollis was once again selected to fight for her country in the men's team event. Women's participation in official events prior to the 2000 11th WKC may be a surprise to most as it is presumed women only competed in unofficial goodwill competitions.

At the 9th WKC held in France in 1994, the first unofficial women's individual and three-person team events were held. There were 70 competitors in the individual competition. Also included in the programme was a 15-a-side goodwill team match between a European demonstration team made up of women and men, and a Japanese women's team. Liz Dutton representing Great Britain scored a roof raising *debana-kote* against her Japanese opponent, and fellow teammate Frank Dutton won his match 2-1. The final match finished with *hikiwake* between Italian representative Rossi and Sato Rie. Only three points were scored against the Japanese women who won 12-1. This match was held to demonstrate the power of Japanese women's kendo against European women and men.

In 1997 at the 10th WKC held in Japan, the women's section was starting to resemble an organised competition. Although the women's competition was still unofficial, female competitor's photographs were included in the programme and their results were recorded. The team event consisted of three-person teams, and countries that were able to field more than one team could enter a maximum of two. Individual and team matches were *sanbon-shōbu* and three minutes in duration. Prizes were awarded to the top four places, as well as fighting spirit awards for the team and individual matches.

The women's event was semi-official at the 11th WKC (U.S.A., 2000) and official from the 12th WKC held in Scotland in 2003. Since 2000 the Japanese women's team have dominated the competition. Except for the 14th WKC held in Brazil in 2009, when E. Takashina (Brazil) took third-place, the Japanese women have also secured all the top four places in the individual event since 2000. The Japanese women's team continues to outclass almost every country, except for Korea, with skill and tenacity which has been an inspiration to many male and female practitioners alike. Although the Korean women's teams have challenged Japan in the finals since 2003, they are yet to reach the same level of dexterity and experience that the Japanese women's team possesses. Other than Korea, nations rich in Japanese kendo heritage such as Brazil, Canada and U.S.A. have finished in the top four of the team

Sue Lytollis as a member of the New Zealand men's team.

The Japanese women's team about to face the Korean team in the first official women's team final at the 12th WKC.

event. In the past 10 years European women's kendo has also developed fairly rapidly where finally in 2006 a European nation, Germany, broke into the top four in the team competition, a feat they repeated in 2012.

Although the level of women's international competition kendo has been developing consistently since the 10th WKC in 1997, the disparity in the level between the Japanese women's team and most other countries is wider than in men's international kendo. A former Japanese team member explained that the reason for this is because the Japanese women have been training at the same intensity as their male counterparts for quite some years, unlike women from most other countries. Aside from the professionalism of the Japanese women's kendo team, there are a few other pressing points that are contributing to the slow development of women's kendo outside of Japan. After reviewing the structure of the WKC women's competition events, it seems that the FIK is expressing indifference towards the development of international women's kendo.

There are several issues with the way that the WKC women's competition is formatted that marginalise women and create unequal opportunities. First, at the WKC the women's *shiai* are four minutes in duration compared to five minutes for the men. At the All Japan Women's Kendo Championships, all matches are five minutes but become 10 minutes from the fourth round onwards, the same as the men's championships. It does not make sense that women's matches at the WKC are one minute shorter, especially given that women competitors are as physically conditioned as their male counterparts. The difference of one minute in *shiai* duration does more than just reflect reduced time allocated to women's competition. An issue with four-minute matches at the WKC is that this *shiai* time is then replicated in most other countries, which in turn perpetuates the myth of women's physical inferiority.

Second, at the WKC the women's team event and individual event are held on the same day. This format

makes it very difficult for women who are competing in both events to be appropriately prepared. Finally, at the WKC all of the *shinpan* are male. At the top kendo competitions for women in Japan (the AJWKC and the All Japan Inter-prefectural Competition), all *shinpan* are women. There are several skilled female *shinpan* in Japan who would most certainly qualify to adjudicate at the WKC. For the WKC to progress without further gender discrimination, the above points need to be addressed and amended by the FIK.

I would like to sincerely thank Donatella Castelli-sensei, Hyun Hong Wright (Cho)-sensei, Sue Lytollis-sensei, and Liz Dutton-sensei for their valuable contributions to this article.

Japan's Yuka Tsubota vs. S-M. Lim of Korea.

The 11th
World Kendo Championships

@ Santa Clara, CA USA

March 24-26, 2000   By Jeffrey Marsten

Imagine my surprise when I received the request to do a short write-up on hosting the WKC for Kendo World. Occasionally in nightmares I reflect back on that adventure…

In my capacity as the president of AUSKF (All United States Kendo Federation), I was approached in September 1997 at the 10th WKC in Kyoto, Japan, by the International Kendo Federation (FIK) leadership since the America Zone was up next in the WKC hosting rotation. Honestly, I was very sceptical of the AUSKF hosting the event since we were a new organisation, not wealthy, and still learning about ourselves. The AUSKF had been formed by dissolving the KFUSA (Kendo Federation of the U.S.A.) and the BKR (Beikoku Kendo Renmei). This happened in 1995, and we were structurally quite different from our predecessors. My scepticism was based on the fact that this would be the first time the AUSKF would organise

and host an event. The national championships, which is on a three-year cycle like the WKC, is hosted by one of our regional member federations. They provide most of the logistics and the AUSKF provides the tournament structure. In the Northern California Kendo Federation I knew I had a volunteer to be the host federation for a lot of the local logistics, since their president had volunteered when the "rumour" went around that the FIK wanted the AUSKF to host.

We were officially awarded the 11th WKC in April 1997, and preparations began the following November. Something massive was on the horizon: 1999 would be the AUSKF national championships followed in less than a year by the WKC. In order to prepare for the WKC, we held the AUSKF national championships in Las Vegas, where there was no local kendo population. This meant that volunteers from all over the U.S.A. would have to step up. It was the worst

Jeff Marsten (front row, fourth from right) with officials at the 11th WKC.

national championships ever, and if something could go wrong, it did. Financially it was a bust, but it actually hit the projected cost spot on. The silver lining was how much we actually learned by doing this.

I took several actions to correct the problems, like implementing a clear chain of command and issuing specific job assignments. The only real place where we had problems was in fund-raising. However, due to some generous benefactors, we managed to make it through. We actually hit the predicted loss, just like the national championships, but we still ended up with more money in the bank than both the KFUSA and BKR had brought in combined. This was significant, despite some rock throwers, because we had no major expenses for the next couple of years, and could build our financial reserves back up.

We received lots of compliments on how smoothly the tournament ran, part of which was due to Arnold Matsuda, Richard Hill and Bob Matsueda. The three of them really pulled together the logistics behind the scenes. The other part was due to the more than 50 volunteers who showed up from all over the country to help out. The volunteers received a t-shirt and our thanks, but covered all their own expenses since AUSKF did not have the money to do it.

The greatest part for me personally was being on the FIK Board of Directors and the personal relationships I built during this time. The 2nd WKC was hosted by KFUSA in 1973, and there were 16 participating countries; the 11th WKC had 35 countries participating—a great improvement.

11th World Kendo Championships

Location: Santa Clara, U.S.A.

Venue: Santa Clara University

Date: March 24–26, 2000

Participating Federations: (36) Argentina, Aruba, Australia, Austria, Belgium, Brazil, Canada, Chinese Taipei, Finland, France, Germany, Great Britain, Hawaii, Hong Kong, Hungary, Italy, Japan, Korea, Macao, Malaysia, Mexico, Netherlands, New Zealand, Norway, Portugal, Romania, Russia, Singapore, South Africa, Spain, Sweden, Switzerland, Thailand, U.S.A., Venezuela, Yugoslavia

Competitor Breakdown: 30 men's teams, 19 women's teams, 166 men (ind.), 92 women (ind.)

Results:

Men's Team:
1st	Japan
2nd	Korea
3rd	Canada
	Brazil

Men's Individual:
1st	N. Eiga (JPN)
2nd	K. Takenaka (JPN)
3rd	T. Someya (JPN)
	S-S. Hong (KOR)

Women's Team:
1st	Japan
2nd	Brazil
3rd	U.S.A. / Canada

Women's Individual:
1st	T. Kawano (JPN)
2nd	K. Baba (JPN)
3rd	H. Yano (JPN)
	S. Asahina (JPN)

Debut Federations: Aruba, Macau, Russia, Thailand

Trivia:

- The maximum number of competitors for each country was reduced from 12 to 10.
- Japan had a close call against Canada. Senpō and Jihō drew, Canadian Chūken beat his Japanese opponent 2-1, the Japanese Fukushō won 2-0, and the Japanese Taishō won 2-0 to seal the deal for Japan, but only after one flag went up for a *dō* strike for Canada.
- The final between Japan and Korea was also very close. In the end, Japanese Taishō Takahashi Hideaki scored a *kote* and a *dō* against J-K. Kim to clinch the team competition for Japan.
- J-K. Kim was nursing a torn calf muscle all day.
- Eiga Naoki won the individual competition for Japan against his compatriot Takenaka Kentarō. Eiga makes it a double later in the year when he also won the AJKC.
- The Women's event was semi-official.
- FIK decides to cease playing the national anthem and raising the flag of the winner.

The Japanese men's team.

The victorious Japanese women's team and top four individual competitors.

U.S.A.'s Chris Yang scores a *tsuki* against Korea's N-C. Seo in the first round of the men's individual competition.

Suguru Asaoka of Canada scores a *de-gote* against Japan's Hirao Yasushi to win the Chūken match in the semi-final.

Brett Smith of Australia goes for *men* against Brazil's Flavio Hayashi in the quarter-final of the men's team competition. After the match ended 2-2, Brazil progressed on the basis of more *ippon* scored.

In the final of the women's individual competition, Kawano Tomoko of Japan scores *men* against compatriot Baba Keiko to win.

Men's Team Best-16

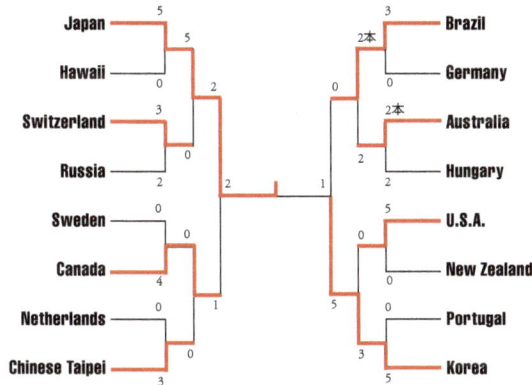

Japan	5	
Hawaii	0	5
		2
Switzerland	3	
Russia	2	0
Sweden	0	
Canada	4	0
		1
Netherlands	0	
Chinese Taipei	3	0

2本 — Brazil 3 / Germany 0
2本 — Australia 2 / Hungary 2
U.S.A. 5 / New Zealand 0
Portugal 3 / Korea 5

Women's Team Best-16

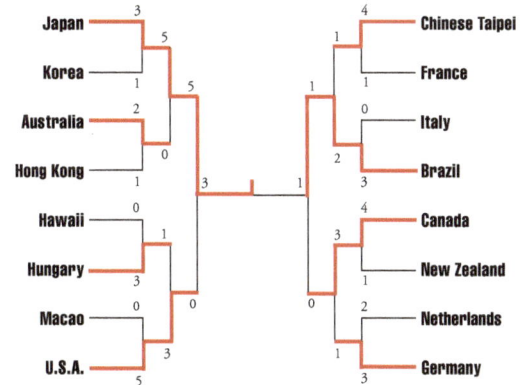

Japan	3	
Korea	1	5
		5
Australia	2	
Hong Kong	1	0
Hawaii	0	
Hungary	3	1
		0
Macao	0	
U.S.A.	5	3

Chinese Taipei 4 / France 1
Italy 0 / Brazil 3
Canada 4 / New Zealand 1
Netherlands 2 / Germany 3

Men's Individual Best-16

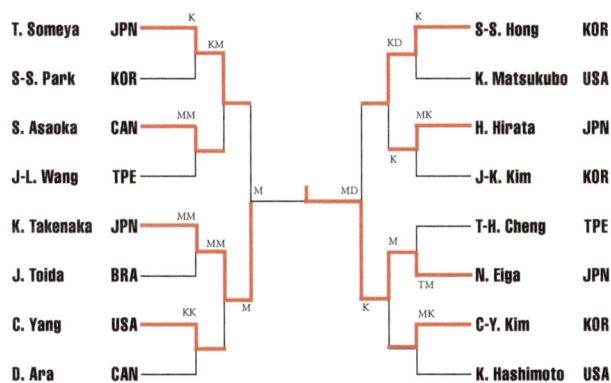

T. Someya	JPN		S-S. Hong	KOR
S-S. Park	KOR		K. Matsukubo	USA
S. Asaoka	CAN		H. Hirata	JPN
J-L. Wang	TPE		J-K. Kim	KOR
K. Takenaka	JPN		T-H. Cheng	TPE
J. Toida	BRA		N. Eiga	JPN
C. Yang	USA		C-Y. Kim	KOR
D. Ara	CAN		K. Hashimoto	USA

Women's Individual Best-16

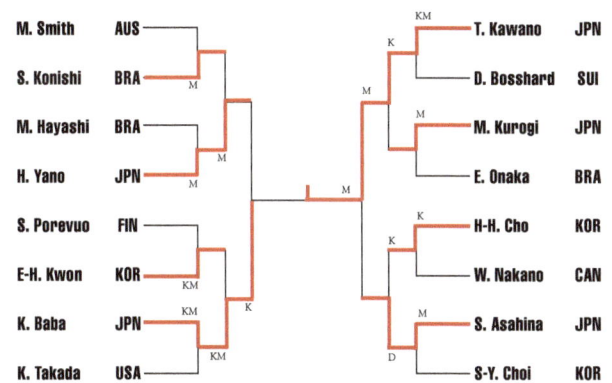

M. Smith	AUS		T. Kawano	JPN
S. Konishi	BRA		D. Bosshard	SUI
M. Hayashi	BRA		M. Kurogi	JPN
H. Yano	JPN		E. Onaka	BRA
S. Porevuo	FIN		H-H. Cho	KOR
E-H. Kwon	KOR		W. Nakano	CAN
K. Baba	JPN		S. Asahina	JPN
K. Takada	USA		S-Y. Choi	KOR

The Nihon Kendo Kata at the 12th WKC.

Recollections of Organising a WKC

By Paul Budden

The 12th WKC in Glasgow 2003 holds special memories for me. It was a time of extreme focus, many meetings, and a huge workload after we had initially agreed to host the event some three years prior. In order to smooth the running of the championships, as well as safeguard the British Kendo Association (BKA) from the financial risks from the large overhead cost, it had been decided that a limited company should be formed: 12th WKC Ltd. The three directors of 12th WKC were: John Howell, Championship Chairman and Financial controller; Geoff Salmon, Championship Marketing and Sponsorship; and myself, Paul Budden, Championship Co-ordinator.

We assembled a large body of BKA personnel, but knew this would not be enough to run the four *shiai-jō*. I therefore contacted various individuals I had worked with at EKCs around Europe to help form the *shiai-jō* management teams. Belgium, France, Germany, Holland, Italy and Switzerland contributed personnel, and without their outstanding contributions it would have proved very difficult to run the WKC. Their

accommodation and food would be paid for, but not their travel expenses. Perhaps a small price to pay for the best seats in the house.

The venue, Kelvin Hall, was small in comparison to both the previous and subsequent WKCs, but the atmosphere was breathtaking, and the size ensured a packed house. The arena was dressed professionally by an experienced exhibition contractor (no names, but I cut a finger) in conjunction with the Kelvin Hall staff. Spectators and competitors were presented with an unforgettable sight as they entered the venue, and the image of the huge championship poster remains very clear in my mind to this day.

The opening ceremony was spectacular. We had experienced initial opposition to the pipe band marching on the *shiai-jō*, even though this was prior to the actual competition starting. Fortunately, common sense prevailed and the crowd and officials went wild when the pipe band burst into the arena. *Shinpan* and officials stood on the tables (including those who

Prince Philip and Queen Elizabeth II with Championship Chairman John Howell.

had earlier made an objection!) to take photos with a barrage of flashes. Flash photography was something that unfortunately prevailed throughout the event, and I forget how many times I had to announce "No flash photography" over and over in the many languages represented. The sword dance also proved to be a crowd-pleaser, and sacrilegious thoughts of someone dancing over swords quickly vanished as the tiny female dancer meticulously strutted her stuff in her kilt.

The high point of the WKC was of course the visit by Queen Elizabeth II and Prince Philip. There are stories to be told, but I might just end up in the Tower if they are repeated. Suffice it to say, I'm sure that Italy's Donatella Castelli remembers the conversation with Prince Philip about her bruises.

The preparation, presentation and overall perception of the WKC were second to none, a sentiment constantly repeated by competitors, officials and spectators from around the world. We still received messages of congratulations and appreciation a month after the event. I think we can say that we achieved our objective of putting on one of the best WKC ever.

There were a few headaches, including pressure from the AJKF/FIK over TV rights that I had sold to a PR company for £100,000. This would have been a very welcome bonus and would have made the event an "L.A. Olympics" in that we would have become profitable. However, we were subsequently told that NHK had prior agreement for broadcast rights, which was something we had not been made aware of in our initial discussions. As far as we knew, we had been given a written contract to run the event carte blanche.

Thankfully I was able to redeem the rights without cost from the PR Company, but it did leave a sour taste in our mouths for some time after.

There were other small problems, such as the IT setup. We had hoped to have a computer program that controlled everything, but these were still early days for computer technology and such ambitious software. It crashed dramatically beyond repair. However, a back-up system was introduced using a simple Excel spreadsheet which worked in conjunction with both hard copy and *shiai-jō* networking. Overall it worked adequately and you never saw the joins.

NHK made a programme of the championships where it was very clear what a big undertaking the 12th WKC actually was, and how well it ran. There had been a few minor setbacks, but overall it ran like clockwork. Someone quipped that it looked rather like a swan swimming—calm and gliding above the water, but with frantic leg movements below making it all happen. Together we wrote history in achieving probably the most successful WKC to date.

There were no recriminations or an autopsy after the event, which we had been led to believe usually happened, and I firmly believe that the AJKF/FIK officials involved may have just been a touch in awe of our organisational skills. Only three main directors had called all of the shots and it had all gone very smoothly. There was also a fantastic climax to an unforgettable team final. Who will ever forget Eiga's final *tsuki*?

The 12th WKC will always be a very hard act to follow.

12th World Kendo Championships

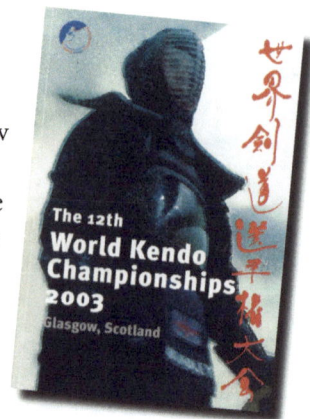

The 12th
World Kendo
Championships
2003
Glasgow, Scotland

Location: Glasgow, Scotland

Venue: Kelvin Hall

Date: July 4–6, 2003

Participating Federations: (41) Andorra, Argentina, Aruba, Australia, Austria, Belgium, Brazil, Canada, Chile, Chinese Taipei, Czech Republic, Denmark, Finland, France, Germany, Great Britain, Hawaii, Hong Kong, Hungary, Ireland, Italy, Japan, Korea, Luxembourg, Macao, Malaysia, Mexico, Netherlands, New Zealand, Norway, Poland, Portugal, Russia, Singapore, South Africa, Spain, Sweden, Switzerland, Thailand, U.S.A., Yugoslavia

Competitor Breakdown: 36 men's teams, 20 women's teams, 188 men (ind.), 115 women (ind.)

Results:

Men's Team:
1st	Japan
2nd	Korea
3rd	U.S.A. / Italy

Men's Individual:
1st	H. Satō (JPN)
2nd	H. Iwasa (JPN)
3rd	M. Satō (JPN)
	K-B. Lim (KOR)

Women's Team:
1st	Japan
2nd	Korea
3rd	Canada
	Chinese Taipei

Women's Individual:
1st	K. Baba (JPN)
2nd	Y. Tsubota (JPN)
3rd	K. Okada (JPN)
	S. Asahina (JPN)

Debut Federations: Andorra, Chile, Ireland

Trivia:
- There were 38 men's teams divided into 8 blocks of 3–6 teams.
- Only the top two teams advanced to the tournament stage, and each team fought two matches in the pools. As with previous WKCs, this system was criticised as being unfair as strong teams ended up being pitted against other strong opponents in the group and were knocked out straightaway. Whereas, some of the weaker teams were able to progress if they were lucky enough not to draw one of the favourites.
- This WKC featured the first fully official women's competition.
- Italy became the first European team to finish in the top four of the men's competition.
- The men's team final was the first to be decided by a play-off (*daihyō-sen*).
- Eiga Naoki scores an epic one-handed *tsuki* to defeat K-N. Kim for Japan to take the championship after a tense 10-minute battle.
- Serving Korea in the dual role of player and coach, K-N. Kim did not fight in the earlier rounds, and seemed to be saving himself for this showdown.
- Veteran Kim had never been beaten by a Japanese player in the team competition before.
- The Korean team lines up for the final bow very slowly. In a fit of rage, the Korean Kantoku infamously snaps his Kantoku flag in two.
- Mikko Salonen (Finland) was only the second European to make the best-8 of the men's individual competition.
- Chris Yang makes the best-8 for the second successive WKC.
- In the women's team competition, Korea and Japan are in the same block for the preliminary rounds. Japan defeats Korea, but both teams advance to the tournament.
- Japan defeats Korea again in the final.
- All but one of the Korean players were students.

Eiga Naoki wins the men's team competition for Japan with that *tsuki*.

Men's Team Best-16

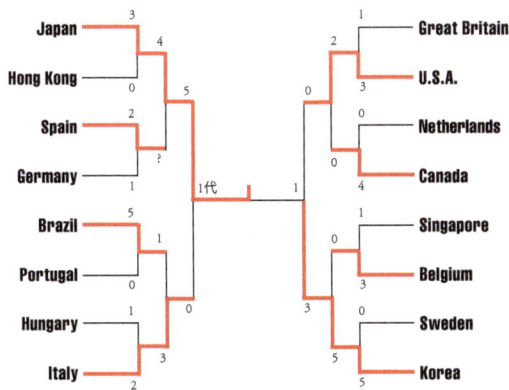

```
Japan        3
                4
Hong Kong    0
                5                        2   Great Britain   1
Spain        2                               U.S.A.          3
                ?                        0
Germany      1                               Netherlands     0
                1代        1                  Canada          4
Brazil       5
                1
Portugal     0
                0                        0   Singapore       1
Hungary      1                               Belgium         3
                3                        3
Italy        2                               Sweden          0
                                         5   Korea           5
```

Women's Team Best-16

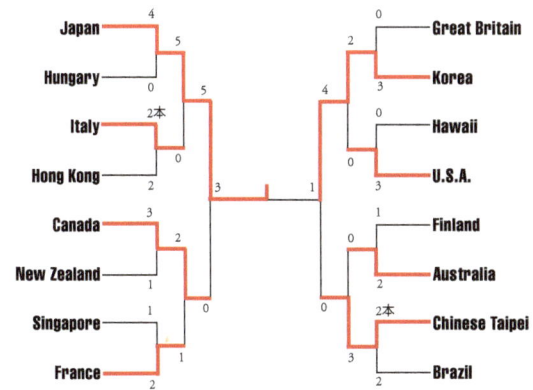

```
Japan        4
                5
Hungary      0
                3                        2   Great Britain   0
Italy        2本                              Korea           3
                                  1      0
Hong Kong    2                               Hawaii          0
                          1                  U.S.A.          3
Canada       3
                2
New Zealand  1
                0                        1   Finland         1
Singapore    1                               Australia       2
                          0              0
France       2                               Chinese Taipei  2本
                                         3   Brazil          2
```

Men's Individual Best-16

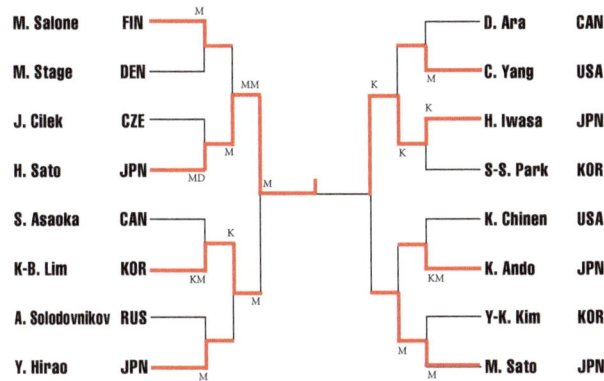

```
M. Salone         FIN    M
                            MM
M. Stage          DEN
J. Cilek          CZE
                            M                     D. Ara       CAN
H. Sato           JPN    MD                        C. Yang      USA
                                     M    K       H. Iwasa     JPN
                                                  S-S. Park    KOR
S. Asaoka         CAN                    KM
                            K                     K. Chinen    USA
K-B. Lim          KOR    KM                        K. Ando      JPN
                            M                      Y-K. Kim     KOR
A. Solodovnikov   RUS                    M        M. Sato      JPN
Y. Hirao          JPN    M
```

Women's Individual Best-16

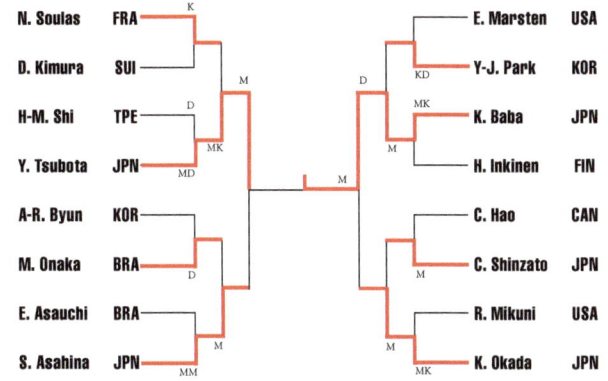

```
N. Soulas   FRA    K
                       K
D. Kimura   SUI
                       M                          E. Marsten   USA
H-M. Shi    TPE    D              D               Y-J. Park    KOR
                       MK             KD          K. Baba      JPN
Y. Tsubota  JPN    MD       M    MK               H. Inkinen   FIN
A-R. Byun   KOR
                       D                          C. Hao       CAN
M. Onaka    BRA                                   C. Shinzato  JPN
                                          M
E. Asauchi  BRA    M                              R. Mikuni    USA
                       MM        MK               K. Okada     JPN
S. Asahina  JPN
```

13th World Kendo Championships

Location: Taipei, Chinese Taipei

Venue: University of Taipei Gymnasium

Date: December 8–10, 2006

Participating Federations: (43) Aruba, Australia, Austria, Belgium, Brazil, Bulgaria, Canada, Chile, Chinese Taipei, Czech Republic, Denmark, Dominican Republic, Finland, France, Germany, Great Britain, Greece, Hawaii, Hong Kong, Hungary, Ireland, Italy, Japan, Korea, Macao, Malaysia, Mexico, Netherlands, New Zealand, Norway, Poland, Portugal, Romania, Russia, Singapore, South Africa, Spain, Sweden, Switzerland, Thailand, U.S.A., Venezuela, Yugoslavia

Competitor Breakdown:
39 men's teams, 21 women's teams, 157 men (ind.), 93 women (ind.)

Results:

Men's Team:	1st	Korea
	2nd	U.S.A.
	3rd	Japan
		Chinese Taipei
Men's Individual:	1st	M. Hōjō (JPN)
	2nd	T. Tanaka (JPN)
	3rd	S-H. Kang (KOR)
		G-H. Oh (KOR)
Women's Team:	1st	Japan

2nd   Korea
3rd   Germany
      Canada

Women's Individual:

1st   S. Sugimoto (JPN)
2nd   K. Komuro (JPN)
3rd   E. Inagaki (JPN)
      M. Shimokawa (JPN)

Debut Federations: Bulgaria, Dominican Republic, Greece

Trivia:

- From this tournament, each federation was allowed a maximum of four representatives in the individuals, down from five.
- The men's teams were divided into 13 blocks of three teams, with only one team progressing from each block to the tournament stage.
- In three blocks (A- Japan, Switzerland, Taiwan; G-U.S.A., Great Britain, Portugal; M–Korea, Canada, France) two teams were allowed to advance.

- This was the first time ever that all of the Japanese men (10 competitors) were policemen.
- U.S.A. had a close match against Canada with Chris Yang scoring two points in the Taishō match to clinch victory the quarterfinal.
- U.S.A. defeats Japan 3–2 in the semi-final. This is the first time Japan has ever lost.
- Head coach (Kakehashi Masaharu) and captain (Seike Kōichi) officially expressed their apologies to Japan for the "loss of honour", taking the brunt of the responsibility on their own shoulders in the AJKF's monthly newsletter *Kensō (February 2007)*.
- Germany became the first European nation to finish in the top four of the women's team competition.
- Guillaume Sicart (France) was the third European to make the best-8 of the men's individual competition.
- Yoneya Yūichi snapped his Achilles tendon in training and is unable to compete in the individuals.

Chris Yang (U.S.A.) faces Nakada Jun in the semi-final.

Marvin Kawabata in the semi-final Taishō match against Seike Koichi (Japan).

Seike Kōichi (Japan) goes for *gyaku-dō* against Marvin Kawabata (U.S.A.).

Marvin Kawabata scores an *ippon* in the semi-final Taishō match against Seike Koichi (Japan).

The Japanese team look distraught after losing the semi-final match against the U.S.A.

Chris Yang leads the U.S.A. team off the *shiai-jō* after defeating Japan.

Korea's W-S. Kim faces Danny Yang in the Jihō match of the final.

Korea's W-S. Kim faces Danny Yang in the Jihō match of the final.

Chris Yang fights for the centre against K-H. Lee.

S-H. Kang tries to find an opening against Fumihide Itokazu.

The Korean and American Taishō battle it out.

The new world champions bow to their opponents before leaving the *shiai-jō*.

The victorious Korean team celebrate.

The victorious Korean team receive the winner's trophy.

Men's Team Best-16

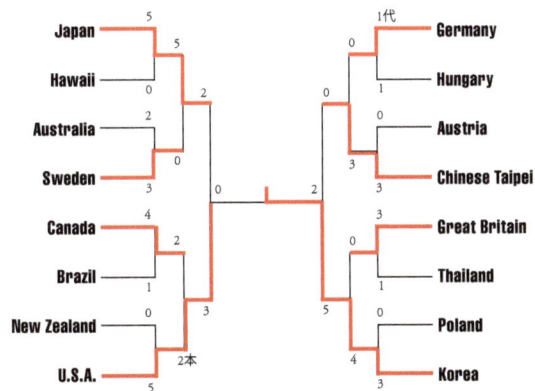

```
Japan      5 ┐
             ├ 5 ┐                    1代  Germany
Hawaii     0 ┘   │                    0 ┌─ Hungary
             ┌ 2 ┤              0 ┌────┤  1
Australia  2 ┐   │                 │   ┌─ Austria
             ├ 0 ┘              3 ┤   3└─ Chinese Taipei
Sweden     3 ┘        0 ─┬─ 2 ─────┤
                         │         │   5┌─ Great Britain
Canada     4 ┐          │         0 ┤ 1└─ Thailand
             ├ 2 ┐       │              └┤
Brazil     1 ┘   │       │           0 ┌─ Poland
             ┌ 3 ┤       │           4 └─ Korea
New Zealand 0┐   │   2本              3
             ├ 5 ┘
U.S.A.     5 ┘
```

Women's Team Best-16

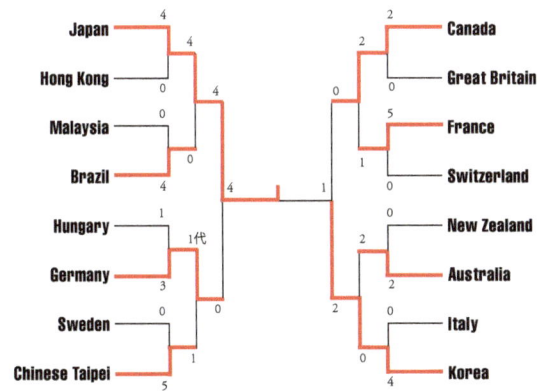

```
Japan       4 ┐
              ├ 4 ┐                   2 ┌─ Canada
Hong Kong   0 ┘   │               0 ┌─┤ 0└─ Great Britain
              ┌ 4 ┤                 │   5┌─ France
Malaysia    0 ┐   │               1 ┤ 1 └─ Switzerland
              ├ 0 ┘       1 ─┬─────┤
Brazil      4 ┘              │     │   2┌─ New Zealand
                    1代       │     2 ┤ 2└─ Australia
Hungary     1 ┐  1代          │       └┤
              ├ 3 ┐           │        0┌─ Italy
Germany     3 ┘   │           │        0└─ Korea
              ┌ 0 ┤           │         4
Sweden      0 ┐   │           │
              ├ 1 ┘
Chinese Taipei 5 ┘
```

Men's Individual Best-16

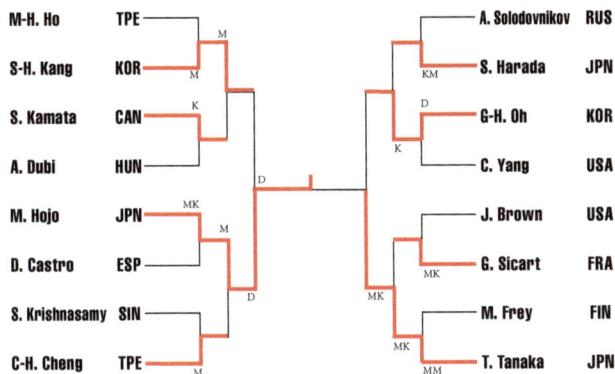

```
M-H. Ho      TPE              M            A. Solodovnikov  RUS
                   M ┐             KM ┌──   S. Harada        JPN
S-H. Kang    KOR     │          D ┌──┤
S. Kamata    CAN   K │            │  K└──   G-H. Oh          KOR
                     ┤          K ┤         C. Yang          USA
A. Dubi      HUN     │   D ──┬───┤
M. Hojo      JPN  MK │       │    │  MK┌──  J. Brown         USA
                   M ┤       │    │ ┌─┤    G. Sicart        FRA
D. Castro    ESP     │     D │    MK│ │     M. Frey          FIN
                     ┘       │    └─┤ MM└── T. Tanaka        JPN
S. Krishnasamy SIN  ┐        │
                   M┘
C-H. Cheng   TPE
```

Women's Individual Best-16

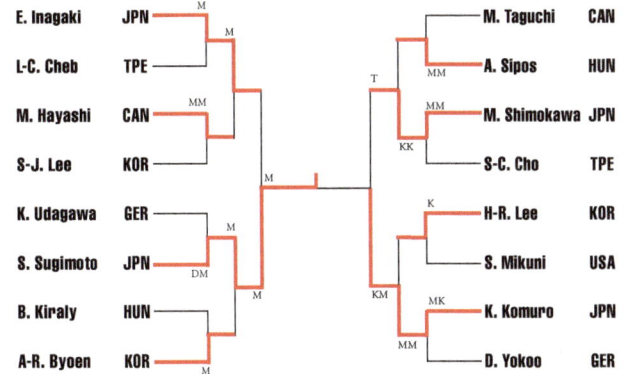

```
E. Inagaki   JPN        M              M. Taguchi   CAN
                  M ┐         MM ┌──   A. Sipos     HUN
L-C. Cheb    TPE    │       T ┌──┤ MM
M. Hayashi   CAN  MM┤         │  ┌──   M. Shimokawa JPN
                    │       KK┤         S-C. Cho     TPE
S-J. Lee     KOR    │  M ──┬──┤
K. Udagawa   GER  M ┤      │  │  K ┌──  H-R. Lee     KOR
                DM ┤       │  │ ┌─┤      S. Mikuni   USA
S. Sugimoto  JPN   │     M │  KM│ │ MK   K. Komuro   JPN
                   ┘       │  └─┤ └────  D. Yokoo    GER
B. Kiraly    HUN  ┐        │  MM
                  M┘       │
A-R. Byoen   KOR
```

14th World Kendo Championships

Location: Sao Paulo, Brazil

Venue: Ginasio Adib Moyses Dib

Date: August 28–30, 2009

Participating Federations:
38–Argentina, Aruba, Australia, Brazil, Canada, Chile, China, Chinese Taipei, Czech Republic, Dominican Republic, Finland, France, Germany, Great Britain, Hawaii, Hong Kong, Hungary, Ireland, Israel, Italy, Japan, Korea, Macau, Malaysia, Mexico, Netherlands, New Zealand, Norway, Poland, Portugal, Romania, Russia, South Africa, Spain, Sweden, Switzerland, U.S.A., Venezuela

Competitor Breakdown: 34 men's teams, 19 women's teams, 143 men (ind.), 99 women (ind.)

Results:

Men's Team:
- 1st Japan
- 2nd U.S.A.
- 3rd Korea
-      Brazil

Men's Individual:
- 1st S. Teramoto (JPN)
- 2nd B-H. Park (KOR)
- 3rd K-H. Lee (KOR)
-      C-K. Choi (KOR)

Women's Team:
- 1st Japan
- 2nd Korea
- 3rd U.S.A.
-      Brazil

Women's Individual:
- 1st Y. Takami (JPN)
- 2nd S. Shōjima (JPN)
- 3rd C. Shinzato (JPN)
-      E. Takashina (BRA)

Debut Federations: Israel, Serbia

Trivia:

- Men's individual winner Teramoto Shōji (Japan) was the only Japanese competitor in the top four.
- Eliete Takashina (Brazil) was the first non-Japanese competitor to finish in the top four of the women's individual competition.
- B-H. Park (Korea) was the first non-Japanese runner-up in the men's individual competition, but was defeated by Teramoto with a men strike.
- Japan and Korea meet in the semi-final of the men's team competition. Japan advances and avenges their loss to the U.S.A. in the previous WKC by beating them in the final 4–0.
- The Sayonara party was awesome!

Photos courtesy of *Kendo Nihon*

Chinese Taipei's Y-Y. Lui scores a crushing *men* against Poland's Rafal Jastak.

Hawaii's Seth Harris faces Kirby Smith (Australia).

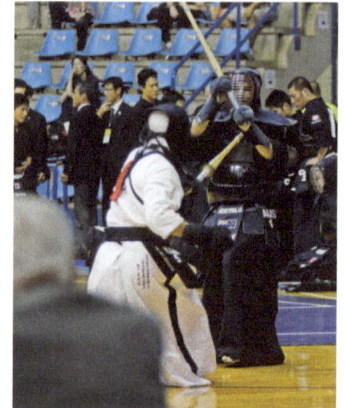

Korea's W-S. Kim goes for *tsuki* against Australia's Kirby Smith.

Teramoto Shōji scores a *men* against Chris Yang in the Taishō match in the team final.

Japan's Kiwada Daiki and Korea's Y-C. Kim get into it in the team event.

The Japanese women's team enjoy their success in the team competition.

Japan's Sakuma Yōko scores *tsuki* against Korea's S-Y. Park in the final of the women's team competition.

Teramoto Shōji and B-H. Park battle for the centre in the final of the men's individual competition.

Uchimura Ryōichi and Italy's Fabrizio Mandia compete in the men's team competition. Mandia wins by two *ippon*.

Men's Team Best-16

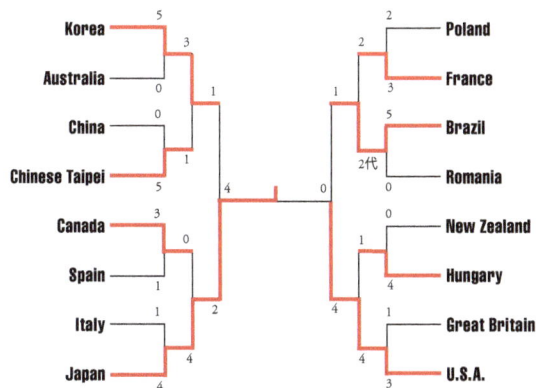

```
Korea          5
                 3
Australia      0
                   1
China          0
                 1              4
Chinese Taipei 5                         0
                                  0
Canada         3
                 0
Spain          1
                   2
Italy          1                4
                 4
Japan          4

Poland         2
                 2
France         3
                   1
Brazil         5
                 2代            0
Romania        0
                                4
New Zealand    0
                 1
Hungary        4
                   4
Great Britain  1                4
                 4
U.S.A.         3
```

Women's Team Best-16

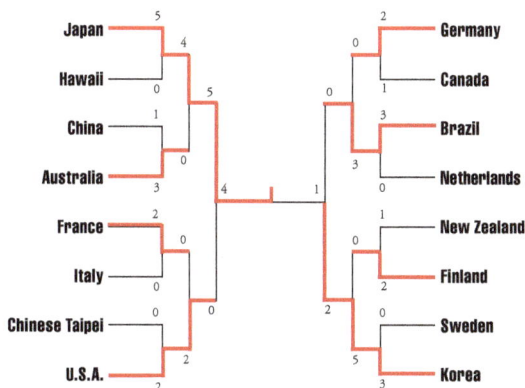

```
Japan          5
                 4
Hawaii         0
                   5
China          1
                 0              4
Australia      3                         1
                                  0
France         2
                 0
Italy          0
                   2
Chinese Taipei 0                2
                 0
U.S.A.         2

Germany        2
                 0
Canada         1
                   3
Brazil         3
                 3              0
Netherlands    0
                                2
New Zealand    1
                 1
Finland        0
                   0
Sweden         0                5
                 5
Korea          3
```

Men's Individual Best-16

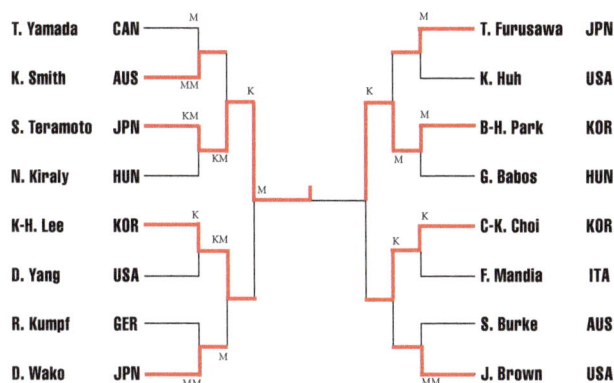

```
T. Yamada      CAN ─ M
                       MM
K. Smith       AUS
                         KM       K
S. Teramoto    JPN ─ KM
                       KM              M
N. Kiraly      HUN

K-H. Lee       KOR ─ K
                       KM
D. Yang        USA
                         M
R. Kumpf       GER
                       MM
D. Wako        JPN ─

                       M
T. Furusawa    JPN ─
                         K
K. Huh         USA
                       M        K
B-H. Park      KOR
                         M
G. Babos       HUN

C-K. Choi      KOR
                       K
F. Mandia      ITA
                         MM
S. Burke       AUS
                       MM
J. Brown       USA
```

Women's Individual Best-16

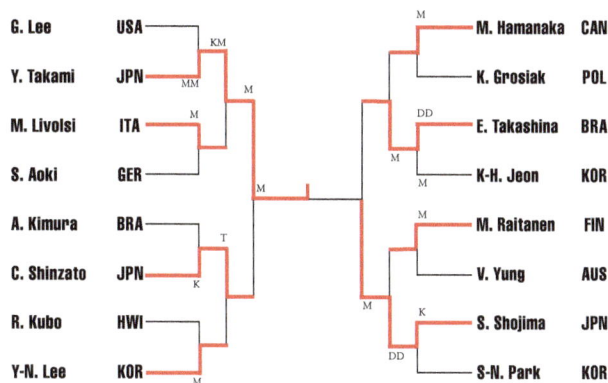

```
G. Lee         USA ─
                       KM
Y. Takami      JPN ─ MM
                         M
M. Livolsi     ITA ─ M
                               M
S. Aoki        GER

A. Kimura      BRA
                       T
C. Shinzato    JPN ─
                         K
R. Kubo        HWI              M

Y-N. Lee       KOR ─            M        DD

                       M
M. Hamanaka    CAN ─
                         DD
K. Grosiak     POL
                       M        M
E. Takashina   BRA ─
                         M
K-H. Jeon      KOR

M. Raitanen    FIN ─
                       M
V. Yung        AUS
                         K
S. Shojima     JPN ─
                       DD
S-N. Park      KOR
```

15th World Kendo Championships

Location: Novara, Italy

Venue: Sporting Village

Date: May 25–27, 2012

Participating Federations: (48) Argentina, Aruba, Australia, Austria, Belgium, Brazil, Bulgaria, Canada, Chile, China, Chinese Taipei, Czech Republic, Ecuador, Finland, France, Germany, Great Britain, Greece, Hawaii, Hong Kong, Hungary, Ireland, Israel, Italy, Japan, Korea, Latvia, Lithuania, Macau, Malaysia, Mexico, Montenegro, Netherlands, New Zealand, Norway, Poland, Portugal, Romania, Russia, Serbia, Singapore, South Africa, Spain, Sweden, Switzerland, Thailand, U.S.A., Venezuela

Competitor Breakdown: 47 men's teams, 30 women's teams, 190 men (ind.), 131 women (ind.)

Results:

Men's Team:	1st	Japan
	2nd	Korea
	3rd	Hungary
		U.S.A.

Men's Individual:	1st	S. Takanabe (JPN)
	2nd	W-S. Kim (KOR)
	3rd	T-H. Kim (KOR)
		K. Furukawa (JPN)

Women's Team:	1st	Japan
	2nd	Korea
	3rd	Germany
		Brazil

Women's Individual:		
	1st	Y. Sakuma (JPN)
	2nd	K. Kurokawa (JPN)
	3rd	S. Shōdai (JPN
		M. Kawagoe (JPN)

Debut Federations: Ecuador, Latvia, Lithuania, Montenegro, Serbia

Trivia:
- Takanabe Susumu of Japan scores a decisive *tsuki* in the final to win a closely fought match against the Korean W-S. Kim.
- Tange from Belgium is the first of his countrymen to ever reach the best-8.
- Japan beats Korea in the final of the women's team competition 1-0. It is the closest margin ever for the women.
- Hungary is the second European team in history to place third in the men's team competition.

- The U.S.A. has a close fought match with Italy in the men's team competition but defeats the home team to advance and take on Korea. The match goes to a decider between the two Taishō. Chris Yang scores men against the Korean Taishō, but is beaten 2-1.
- Korea take on Japan in the final, yet again.
- Many spectators seemed dissatisfied with some of the *shinpan* calls, and raucous booing ensued. (Some of the booing was aimed at the booers.)
- Some of the Korean competitors also openly expressed their dissatisfaction.
- Japan eventually wins the match, but many in Japan and elsewhere criticise the lacklustre way in which it was won.

In the Senpō match, Uchimura Ryōichi (Japan) scores *men* against J-Y. Jo (Korea).

Japan's Sakuma Yōko scores a *tsuki* against K-H. Jeon of Korea in the Fukushō match of the women's team competition.

Takanabe Susumu wins the men's individual competition with a *tsuki* against W-S. Kim.

Men's Team Best-16

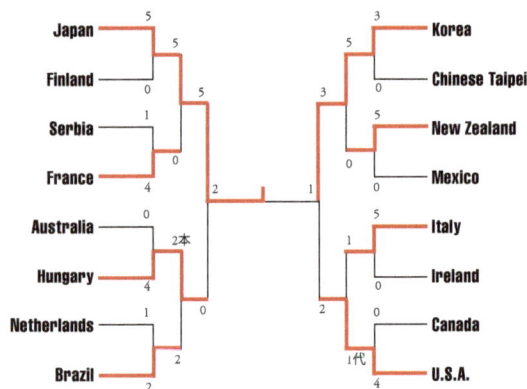

Japan	5		
Finland	0	5	
Serbia	1	5	
France	4	0	2
Australia	0		2本
Hungary	4		0
Netherlands	1	2	
Brazil	2		

Korea	3		
Chinese Taipei	0	5	
New Zealand	5	3	
Mexico			1
Italy	5	1	
Ireland	0	2	
Canada	0		1代
U.S.A.	4		

Women's Team Best-16

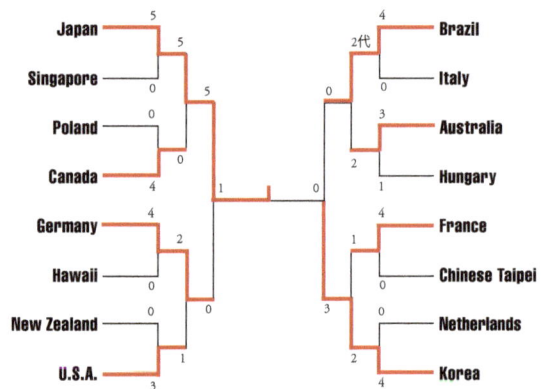

Japan	5		
Singapore	0	5	
Poland	0		1
Canada	4	1	0
Germany	4		
Hawaii	0	2	
New Zealand		0	1
U.S.A.	3		

Brazil	4		
Italy	0	2代	
Australia	3	0	
Hungary	1	2	
France	4		3
Chinese Taipei	0	1	
Netherlands	0	2	
Korea	4		

Men's Individual Best-16

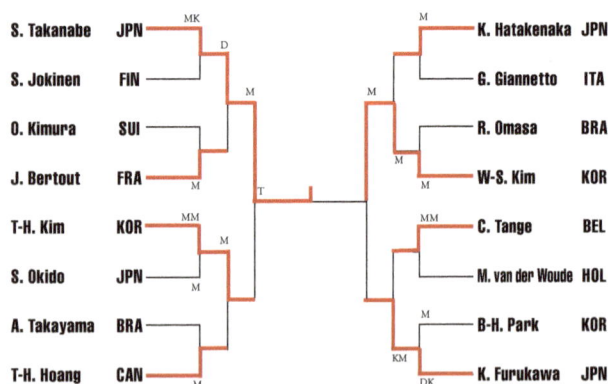

S. Takanabe	JPN	
S. Jokinen	FIN	
O. Kimura	SUI	
J. Bertout	FRA	
T-H. Kim	KOR	
S. Okido	JPN	
A. Takayama	BRA	
T-H. Hoang	CAN	

K. Hatakenaka	JPN	
G. Giannetto	ITA	
R. Omasa	BRA	
W-S. Kim	KOR	
C. Tange	BEL	
M. van der Woude	HOL	
B-H. Park	KOR	
K. Furukawa	JPN	

Women's Individual Best-16

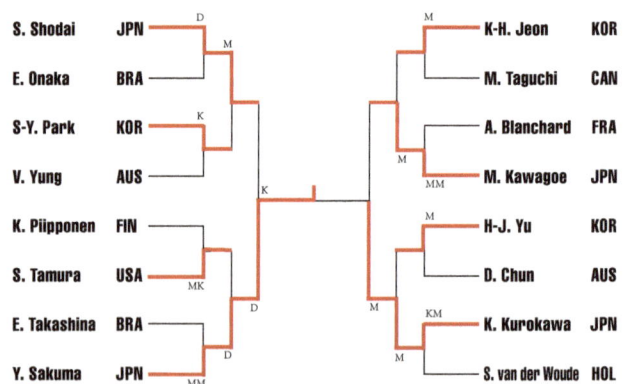

S. Shodai	JPN	
E. Onaka	BRA	
S-Y. Park	KOR	
V. Yung	AUS	
K. Piipponen	FIN	
S. Tamura	USA	
E. Takashina	BRA	
Y. Sakuma	JPN	

K-H. Jeon	KOR	
M. Taguchi	CAN	
A. Blanchard	FRA	
M. Kawagoe	JPN	
H-J. Yu	KOR	
D. Chun	AUS	
K. Kurokawa	JPN	
S. van der Woude	HOL	

An Examination of *Yūkō-datotsu* Scored at the 15th World Kendo Championships in Italy

MUTOH Ken-ichiro*, TAKAHASHI Kentaro**, SAITO Makoto***, OTSUKA Mayumi****, SASAKI Harumitsu****, AMANO Satoshi****, YOSHIMURA Tetsuo *SEIKEI Univ., **KANTO-GAKUIN Univ., ***SENSHU Univ., ****TOKAI Univ.

1. Introduction

At the 16th World Kendo Championships (16WKC) being held in May 2015, 56 countries and regions will be participating—the most ever—and it could be said that the international popularisation of kendo is progressing steadily. However, there are almost no materials that show how kendo is being spread, especially in terms of technique. Therefore, the subject of this study is the 15th World Kendo Championships (15WKC) held in Novara, Italy, in 2012, and it will examine the targets (*datotsu-bui*) of the valid strikes (*yūkō-datotsu*) scored, and will classify the *waza* used by country. By focusing on *yūkō-datotsu* we will be able to understand trends in the *waza* used by competitors from each country. Through understanding these trends, the purpose of this paper is to serve in the examination of the international spread of kendo.

2. Survey Method

2-1. Subject of Investigation

The subject of this investigation are matches that were recorded during the 15WKC held in Novara, Italy, from 25-27 May, 2015. A total of 52 countries and regions participated in this competition. In the men's tournament, there were teams from 47 countries and regions, and 190 competitors in the individual competition. In the women's competition, there were teams from 30 countries and regions and 132 competitors in the individual competition. A total of 1047 matches took place, the breakdown of which follow:

- Individual matches: 252 men's; 178 women's
- Team matches: 331 men's (66 team matches with one *daihyō-sen*); 286 women's (57 team matches with one *daihyō-sen*)

The matches that were recorded and are the subject of this study are as follows:

- Total: 1028 matches (98.2%)
- Men's: 575 matches (98.6%)—individual matches 245 (97.2%); team matches 330 (99.7%)
- Women's: 453 matches (97.6%)—individual matches 171 (96.1%); team matches 282 (98.6%)

2-2. Survey Method

From the video of matches that were recorded, *yūkō-datotsu* were classified according to the "Classification of Waza" found in the Kendo Teaching Guidelines, published by the All Japan Kendo Federation, and were tabulated depending on gender and country. In order to limit the amount of match data tabulated for men, women and country, matches were not divided into those that did or did not have *enchō*, nor whether they were team or individual, but by the *yūkō-datotsu* scored in those matches. An analysis of the many *waza* usedby the top-ranked countries and men and women was carried out.

Then the men's and women's results in the 15WKC were separated, and then the trends for the top-ranked countries were worked out and the many successful *waza* counted. "Top-ranked country" refers to teams that finished in the best-8 and above. These teams were chosen because their number of matches was high and sufficient data could be analysed. Furthermore, the men were compared with the *yūkō-datotsu* scored in the 60th (2012) and 61st (2013) All Japan Kendo Championships, and the women compared with the 51st (2012) and 52nd (2013) All Japan Women's Kendo Championships. Additionally, for each of the team competition finalists (Japan and Korea) in the men's and women's tournaments, the results of the league stage, the early tournament rounds (rounds 1 and 2), and the later tournament rounds (individual competition best-16 and above; team competition semi-finals and final), were tabulated and compared. (Statistical processing was used in this study so only results with a difference greater than 5% were employed.)

3. Results and Discussion

In the charts and tables, the types of *waza* are coloured as follows: *shikake-waza* = blue; *hiki-waza* = red; *ōji-waza* = green; *hansoku* = purple. The *datotsu-bui* are coloured as follows: *men* = blue; *kote* = red; *dō* = green; *tsuki* = purple. This colour scheme is also used in the background of the charts.

3-1. The Men's Competition

3-1-1.   Overview of the Men's Competition

When the *waza* were classified into different groups for the entire men's competition, 67.72% were *shikake-waza* (*hiki-waza* is classified separately), 13.44% were *hiki-waza*, and 17.41% were *ōji-waza*. For *datotsu-bui*, 61.57% were *men*, 30.48% were *kote*, 7.44% were *dō*, and 0.52% were *tsuki*. These are for the team and individual competitions combined, and are represented in Tables 1, and 2, and Figures 1 and 2.

Table 1. Classification of *yūkō-datotsu* waza seen at the 15WKC in the men's competition

	No. of Matches Filmed (Total No. of Matches)	No. of waza analysed	Shikake-waza (excl. Hiki-waza)	Hiki-waza	Ōji-waza	Hansoku
Men's All	575	982	665	132	171	14
	(583)		67.72%	13.44%	17.41%	1.43%
Men's Ind.	245	396	269	49	67	11
	(252)		67.93%	12.37%	16.92%	2.78%
Men's Team	330	586	396	83	104	3
	(331)		67.58%	14.16%	17.75%	0.51%

Table 2. Classification of *yūkō-datotsu datotsu-bui* seen at the 15WKC in the men's competition

Total	968	596	295	72	5
		61.57%	30.48%	7.44%	0.52%
Shikake-waza (excl. Hiki-waza)	665	385	264	11	5
		39.77%	27.27%	1.14%	0.52%
Hiki-waza	132	96	15	21	0
		9.92%	1.55%	2.17%	0.00%
Ōji-waza	171	115	16	40	0
		11.88%	1.65%	4.13%	0.00%

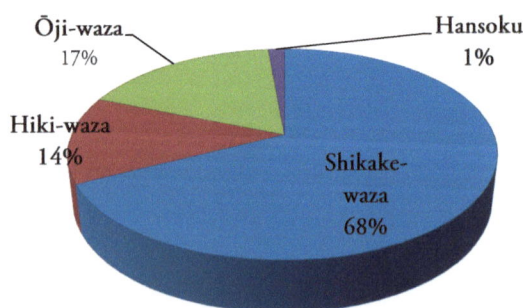

Fig. 1. Classification of all *yūkō-datotsu waza* seen at the 15WKC in the men's competition

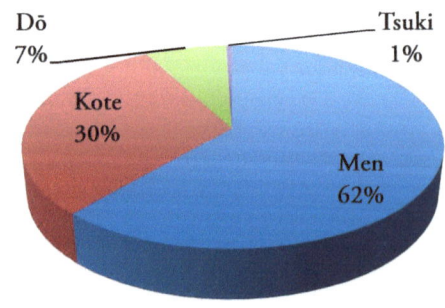

Fig. 2. Classification of all *yūkō-datotsu datotsu-bui* seen at the 15WKC in the men's competition

This data was then compared with that for the *waza* and *datotsu-bui* at the 6th World Kendo Championships (hereafter, 6WKC), as well as the 60th and 61st All Japan Kendo Championships (2012 and 2013 respectively). (See Figures 3, 4)

In a study of the 6WKC (Hirakawa Nobuo, "An Analysis of the 6th World Kendo Championships", 1985), the number of *hiki-waza* was small, and it was included with *shikake-waza*. Therefore, even though an exact comparison cannot be made, the number was considerably larger at the 15WKC. It could be said that because it was classified separately, the number of *hiki-waza* has increased. Also, the ratio of *ōji-waza* could be said to be increasing, and for the *datotsu-bui*, *men-waza* was the main type.

Next, when compared with the All Japan Kendo Championships, there were more *hiki-waza* and less *ōji-waza* observed at the 15WKC. Also, the number of *men-waza* was extremely high. For the two All Japan Kendo Championships, the average age of the competitors was 29.85 years, and the average dan grade was 5.24. First, there is a difference in competitor dan grade and years of experience, which is arguably why such a difference might appear. Also, in the All Japan Kendo Championships, all of the *shinpan* are 8-dan, but this is not the case in the WKC. Therefore, there could be a difference in the way judgements are made, and consequently this could affect the competitors' choice of *waza*.

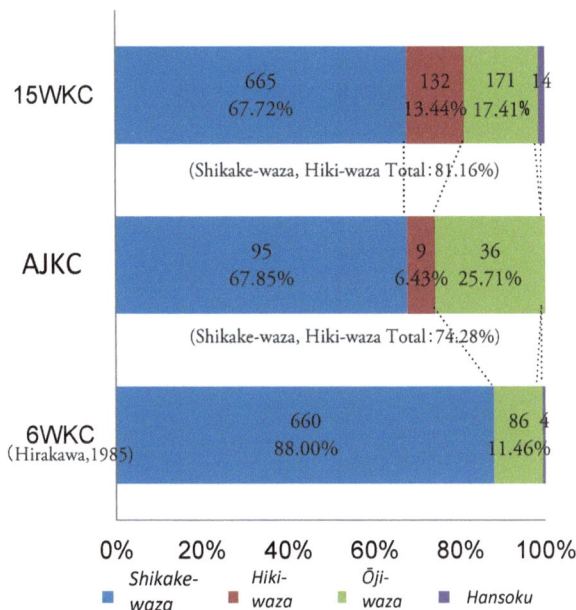

Fig. 3. Classification of *yūkō-datotsu waza* in all of the 15WKC men's matches, 60th and 61st AJKC, and 6WKC

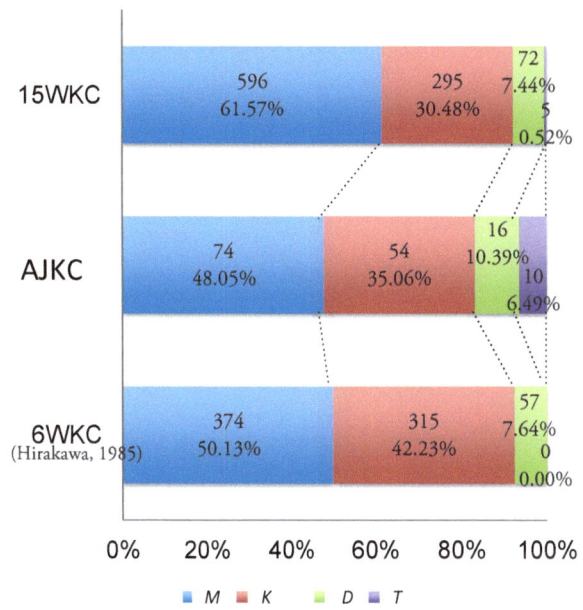

Fig. 4. Classification of *yūkō-datotsu datotsu-bui* in all of the 15WKC men's matches, 60th and 61st AJKC, and 6WKC

Table 3. Number of *yūkō-datotsu* for and against the top-ranked men's countries at the 15WKC

Team	Individual	Country/Region	Total No. of Matches	Individual	Team	Ippon For	Ippon Against	Ippon Difference	Ippon Dif./No. of Matches
Winner	Winner 3rd Best-8 Best16	Japan	60	25	35	92	10	82	1.37
2nd	2nd 3rd Best-16	Korea	52	22	30	72	17	55	1.06
3rd		U.S.A.	35	9	26	41	19	22	0.63
		Hungary	36	11	25	43	29	14	0.39
Best-8	Best-16	Italy	35	14	21	45	10	35	1.00
	Best-16 Best-16	Brazil	37	17	20	42	17	25	0.68
		New Zealand	31	11	20	33	21	12	0.39
	Best-8	France	33	13	20	32	22	10	0.30

From the above, in the case of male competitors around the world, although they use various *waza* like *hiki-waza* and *ōji-waza*, there are less *ōji-waza* compared to the All Japan Kendo Championships, almost no *tsuki*. *Men-waza* is predominant, so we cannot say yet that various *waza* are being used.

3-1-2. Trends with the Top-Ranked Countries and Regions in the Men's Competition

For the best-8 teams, the number of matches, *ippon* for and against, and the average number of *ippon* scored per match (calculated using the difference between *ippon* for and against), are shown in Table 3; the type of *yūkō-datotsu waza* and *datotsu-bui* are shown in Table 4 as well as Figures 5 and 6.

When the averages of the entire 15WKC are looked at as the current global standard, we can understand the following points about the classification of *waza*:

- Korea used the most *shikake-waza*; the U.S.A., Italy, New Zealand and France used the least
- Japan, Brazil and New Zealand used the most *hiki-waza*
- The U.S.A., Italy and France used the most *ōji-waza*, Japan, Korea and Brazil used the least

The *yūkō-datotsu* targets are as follows:

- Korea, Italy, Brazil and France scored the most *men*, Japan and Hungary scored the least

Table 4. Classification of *yūkō-datotsu waza* and *datotsu-bui* in the top-ranked men's countries at the 15WKC

Country/Region	Classification of *Yūkō-datotsu Waza* Scored				Classification of *Yūkō-datotsu Datotsu-bui*			
	Shikake-waza (excl. Hiki-waza)	Hiki-waza	Ōji-waza		Men	Kote	Dō	Tsuki
Japan	65	21	9		47	30	12	3
	68.42%	22.11%	9.47%		51.09%	32.61%	13.04%	3.26%
Korea	58	8	6		51	17	4	0
	80.56%	11.11%	8.33%		70.83%	23.61%	5.56%	0.00%
U.S.A.	18	4	19		24	12	5	0
	43.90%	9.76%	46.34%		58.54%	29.27%	12.20%	0.00%
Hungary	29	6	8		22	19	1	0
	67.44%	13.95%	18.60%		52.38%	45.24%	2.38%	0.00%
Italy	27	7	11		35	9	1	0
	60.00%	15.56%	24.44%		77.78%	20.00%	2.22%	0.00%
Brazil	27	10	5		30	9	2	1
	64.29%	23.81%	11.90%		71.43%	21.43%	4.76%	2.38%
New Zealand	20	7	6		20	9	4	0
	60.61%	21.21%	18.18%		60.61%	27.27%	12.12%	0.00%
France	19	5	8		22	7	3	0
	59.38%	15.63%	25.00%		68.75%	21.88%	9.38%	0.00%

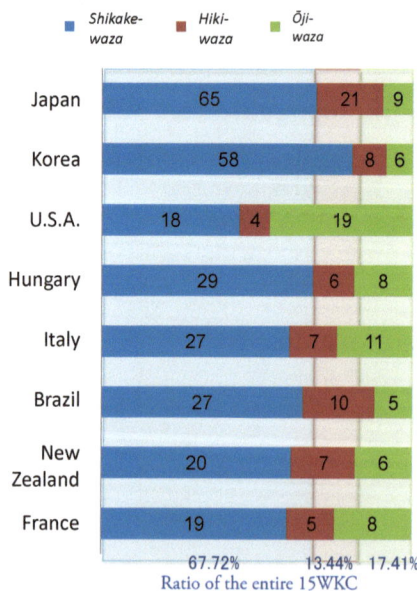

Fig. 5. Comparison of the *yūkō-datotsu waza* between the top-ranked countries and the entire men's competition average

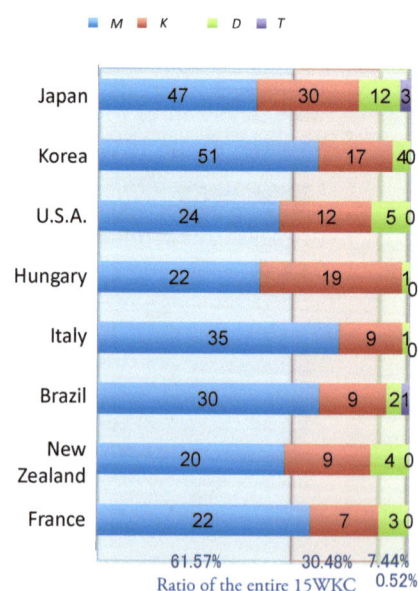

Fig. 6. Comparison of the *yūkō-datotsu datotsu-bui* between the top-ranked countries and the entire men's competition average

- Hungary scored the most *kote*; Korea, Italy, Brazil and France scored the least
- Japan scored the most *dō*, Hungary and Italy scored the least

Next, the top five *waza* observed are shown in Table 5. To begin with, we could collect a large amount of data on the number of *waza*; for example, 58 Korean matches were observed and there were 19 different *waza* used; 65 Japanese matches were observed and 25 different *waza* were used, which is a very large amount.

Furthermore, more than just saying European and American zones, it could be said that each country has its own characteristics. This is not to say that the spread of kendo in each region or zone is not progressing; it could be thought that kendo in each country is developing in its own unique way.

3-1-3. Details Regarding the Countries in the Men's Finals

A detailed examination of the countries represented in both the men's team and individual finals (Japan and Korea) is given in Figure 7. The change in *yūkō-datotsu* in matches in the league stage, the early tournament rounds (1 and 2), and the later tournament rounds (best-16 and above in the individual competition, best-4 and above in the team competition) is shown.

From this it can be understood that Korea used mainly *shikake-waza* and *men-waza* throughout the competition, whereas Japan used mostly *hiki-waza* and *kote-waza* in the early tournament rounds, but in the later tournament rounds used mostly *shikake-waza* with the type of *datotsu-bui* struck being quite even.

That is, if only *yūkō-datotsu* are looked at, considering the many instances of *shikake-waza* that were *yūkō-datotsu*, it is arguable that *ōji-waza* is not developing, and competitors are just defending their opponent's strikes rather than counter-striking. Therefore, that many *shikake-waza* are being scored is not a reflection on the quality of matches, but further research into this trend is needed.

3-1. The Women's Competition

3-1-1.　Overview of the Women's Competition

When looking at the entire women's competition and classifying the *waza* into different groups, 69.13% were *shikake-waza*, 13.23% were *hiki-waza*, and 17.21% were *ōji-waza*. For *datotsu-bui*, 56.43% were *men*, 34.00% were *kote*, 9.43% were *dō*, and 0.14% were *tsuki*. This is shown in Tables 6 and 7, and Figures 8 and 9. *Men-waza* was less, but the type of *waza* and *datotsu-bui* were almost the same percentage as the *men*.

This data has been compared with the *yūkō-datotsu* and *datotsu-bui* observed at the 51st and 52nd All Japan Women's Kendo Championships in 2012 and 2013 respectively. (See Figures 10 and 11). This type of information does not exist for the women's WKC, so we believe that this current data is extremely important.

It is worth noting that for the *yūkō-datotsu* scored in the 15WKC, when compared with the All Japan Women's Kendo Championships, *men* was struck less than *kote*, and the proportion of *shikake-waza*, *hiki-waza*, and *ōji-waza* were almost the same. The main reason for this is there is comparatively no great difference in the composition of the competitors in the men's and women's All Japan Kendo Championships (men: average 29.85 years, average 5.24 dan; women: average 26.4 years; average 4.36 dan). Furthermore, the composition of

Table 5. The top-five *waza* used by the top-ranked countries in the men's competition

Country/Region	Type of *Yuko-datotsu Waza*	*Yūkō-datotsu* Scored by the Top-Ranked Countries					
		1st	2nd	3rd	4th	5th	
Japan	25	Hiki-men	Debana-men	Kote (ippon-uchi)	Debana-kote	Men (ippon-uchi)	Hiki-dō
		15　(16.30%)	13　(14.13%)	12　(13.04%)	10　(10.87%)	5　(5.43%)	
Korea	19	Men (ippon-uchi)	Debana-men	Debana-kote	Kote (ippon-uchi)	Hiki-men	
		20　(27.78%)	9　(12.50%)		6　(8.33%)		
U.S.A.	15	Debana-kote	Kote (ippon-uchi)	Kote-nuki-men	Kote-kaeshi-men	Men-kaeshi-dō	
		6　(14.63%)		5　(12.20%)		4　(9.76%)	
Hungary	15	Debana-kote	Men (ippon-uchi)	Kote (ippon-uchi)	Kote-men (renzoku-waza)	Debana-men	Hiki-men
		9　(20.93%)	7　(16.28%)	6　(13.95%)		3　(6.98%)	
Italy	15	Men (ippon-uchi)	Debana-men	Debana-kote	Hiki-men	Kote (ippon-uchi)	
				6　(13.33%)		5　(11.11%)	
Brazil	15	Hiki-men	Men (ippon-uchi)	Debana-men	Kote (ippon-uchi)	Debana-kote	Katsugi-men
		8　(19.05%)	7　(16.67%)	5　(11.90%)	4　(9.52%)	3　(7.14%)	
New Zealand	9	Debana-kote	Debana-men	Hiki-men	Men (ippon-uchi)	Men-kaeshi-dō	
		8　(24.24%)	7　(21.21%)	5　(15.15%)	4　(12.12%)	3　(9.09%)	
France	14	Debana-men	Men (ippon-uchi)	Debana-kote	Hiki-men	Kote (ippon-uchi) / Kote-men (renzoku-waza) / Kote-nuki-men / Men-kaeshi-dō	
		6　(18.75%)		4　(12.50%)		2　(6.25%)	

Japan

<Classification of *Waza* (No. of)>

	Shikake-waza	Hiki-waza	Ōji-waza
Later Tournament Rounds	20(10)	2(2)	1(1)
Early Tournament Rounds	17(8)	8(3)	4(2)
League Stage	29(12)	11(4)	4(4)

<*Datotsu-bui*>

	M	K	D	T
Later Tournament Rounds	6	8	6	3
Early Tournament Rounds	9	16	3	1
League Stage	11	26	7	0

Korea

<Classification of *Waza* (No. of)>

	Shikake-waza	Hiki-waza	Ōji-waza
Later Tournament Rounds	14(7)	1(1)	2(2)
Early Tournament Rounds	19(7)	3(1)	3(3)
League Stage	24(8)	4(2)	2(2)

<*Datotsu-bui*>

	M	K	D	T
Later Tournament Rounds	14	3	0	0
Early Tournament Rounds	20	3	20	
League Stage	17	11	20	

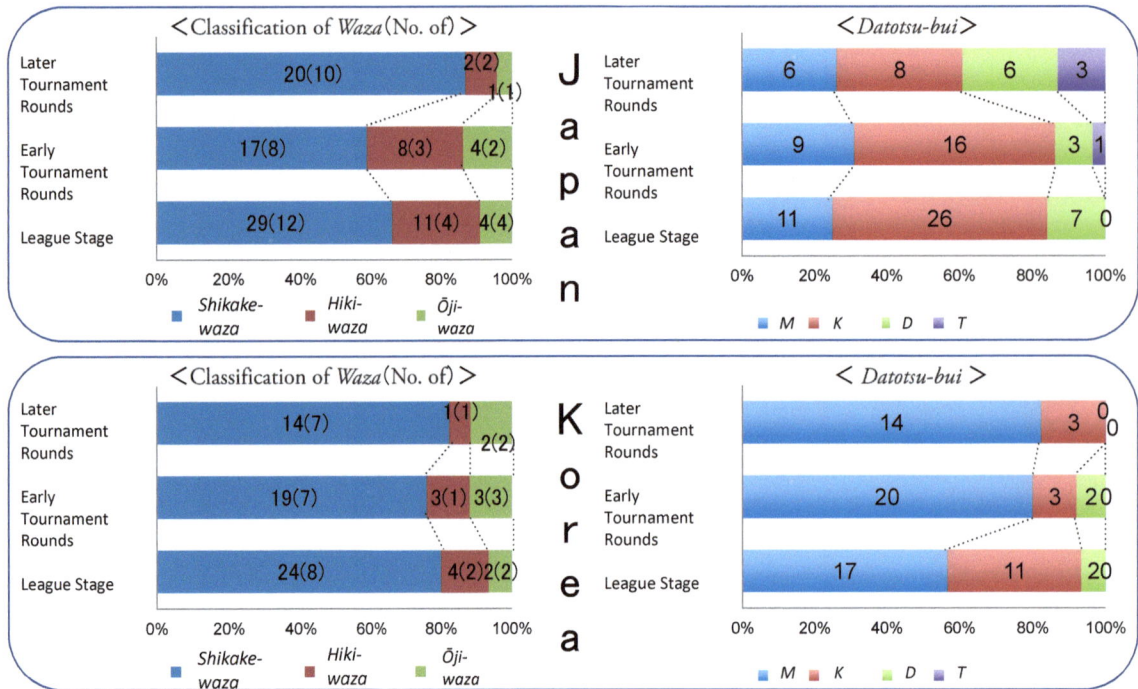

Fig. 7. The changes in *waza* used by the finalists in the different stages of the men's competition

Table 6. Classification of *yūkō-datotsu waza* seen at the 15WKC in the women's competition

	No. of Matches Filmed (Total No. of Matches)	No. of waza analysed	Shikake-waza (excl. Hiki-waza)	Hiki-waza	Ōji-waza	Hansoku
Women's All	453	703	486	93	121	3
	(464)		69.13%	13.23%	17.21%	0.43%
Women's Ind	171	281	185	46	49	1
	(178)		65.84%	16.37%	17.44%	0.36%
Women's Team	282	417	297	45	72	2
	(286)		71.22%	10.79%	17.27%	0.48%

Table 7. Classification of *yūkō-datotsu datotsu-bui* seen at the 15WKC in the women's competition

	No. of Waza (excl. Hansoku)	Men	Kote	Dō	Tsuki
Total	700	395	238	66	1
		56.43%	34.00%	9.43%	0.14%
Shikake-waza (excl. Hiki-waza)	486	254	217	14	1
		36.29%	31.00%	2.00%	0.14%
Hiki-waza	93	58	10	25	0
		8.29%	1.43%	3.57%	0.00%
Ōji-waza	121	83	11	27	0
		11.86%	1.57%	3.86%	0.00%

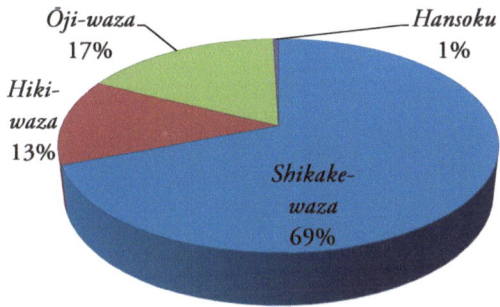

Fig. 8. Classification of *yūkō-datotsu waza* seen at the 15WKC in the women's competition

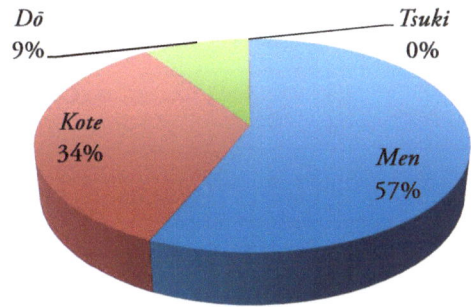

Fig. 9. Classification of *yūkō-datotsu datotsu-bui* seen at the 15WKC in the women's competition

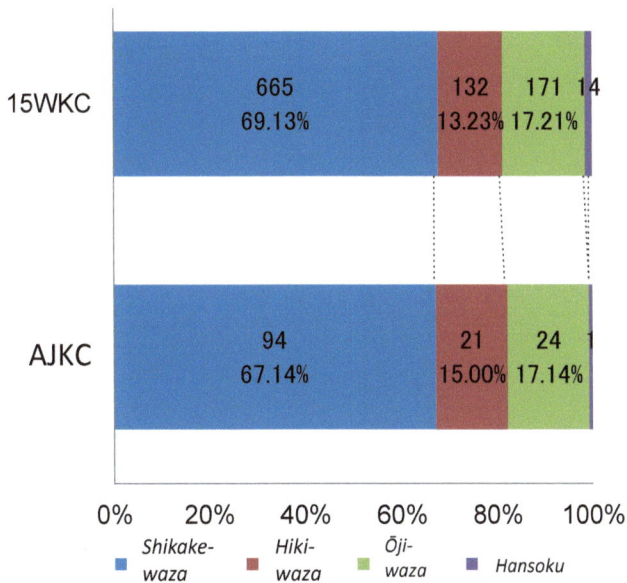

Fig. 10. Classification of valid *waza* in all of the 15WKC women's matches, and the 51st and 52nd AJKC

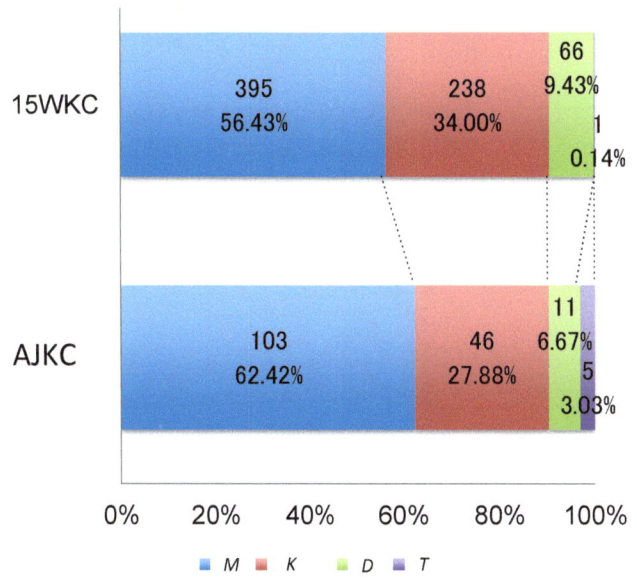

Fig. 11. Classification of *yūkō-datotsu* targets in all of the 15WKC women's matches, and the 51st and 52nd AJKC

shinpan at the All Japan Women's Kendo Championships (at the time) was one 8-dan and two 7-dan, which is similar to the make-up of shinpan at the WKC.

3-1-2. Trends in the Top-Ranked Countries and Regions in the Women's Competition

For the best-8 teams, the number of matches, *ippon* for and against, and the average number of *ippon* scored per match (calculated using the difference between *ippon* for and against), are shown in Table 8; the type of *yūkō-datotsu waza* and *datotsu-bui* are shown in Table 9, as well as Figures 12 and 13.

When the averages of the entire 15WKC are looked at as the current global standard, we can understand the following points about the classification of *waza*:

• Canada and Australia used the most *shikake-waza*;

Brazil, Germany, France and the U.S.A. used the least
• Japan and Brazil used the most *hiki-waza*; Germany used the least
• Germany, France and the U.S.A. used the most *ōji-waza*; Japan, Canada, and Australia used the least

The *yūkō-datotsu datotsu-bui* are as follows:

• Korea scored the most *men*, Germany scored the least
• Canada scored the most *kote*; Japan and Germany scored the least
• Japan, Brazil, and Germany scored the most *dō*; Korea and Canada scored the least

Next, the top five *waza* observed are shown in Table 10. From these results, it can be seen that many of the countries show a similar profile to the men's, and that

Table 8. Number of *yūkō-datotsu* for and against the top-ranked women's countries at the 15WKC

Team	Individual	Country/Region	Total No. of Matches	Individual	Team	*Ippon* For	*Ippon* Against	*Ippon* Difference	*Ippon* Dif./No. of Matches
Winner	Winner 2nd 3rd 3rd	Japan	63	29	34	92	5	87	1.38
2nd	Best-8 Best-8 Best-8	Korea	57	22	35	64	9	55	0.96
3rd	Best-16 Best-16	Brazil	43	13	30	43	16	27	0.63
		Germany	36	11	25	37	18	19	0.53
	Best-16	France	36	11	25	47	20	27	0.75
Best-8	Best-8	U.S.A.	38	13	25	34	10	24	0.63
	Best-16	Canada	38	13	25	34	22	12	0.32
	Best-16 Best-16	Australia	34	13	21	27	28	-1	-0.03

Table 9. Classification of *yūkō-datotsu waza* and *datotsu-bui* in the top-ranked women's countries at the 15WKC

Country/Region	Classification of *Yūkō-datotsu Waza* Scored			Classification of *Yūkō-datotsu Datotsu-bui*			
	Shikake-waza (excl. Hiki-waza)	Hiki-waza	Ōji-waza	Men	Kote	Dō	Tsuki
Japan	57	29	6	53	20	18	1
	61.96%	31.52%	6.52%	57.61%	21.74%	19.57%	1.09%
Korea	49	6	9	41	21	2	0
	76.56%	9.38%	14.06%	64.06%	32.81%	3.13%	0.00%
Brazil	23	11	9	22	13	8	0
	53.49%	25.58%	20.93%	51.16%	30.23%	18.60%	0.00%
Germany	19	2	16	23	7	7	0
	51.35%	5.41%	43.24%	62.16%	18.92%	18.92%	0.00%
France	27	8	12	27	17	3	0
	57.45%	17.02%	25.53%	57.45%	36.17%	6.38%	0.00%
U.S.A.	21	5	8	18	13	3	0
	61.76%	14.71%	23.53%	52.94%	38.24%	8.82%	0.00%
Canada	28	3	3	17	17	0	0
	82.35%	8.82%	8.82%	50.00%	50.00%	0.00%	0.00%
Australia	25	4	2	16	9	2	0
	80.65%	12.90%	6.45%	59.26%	33.33%	7.41%	0.00%

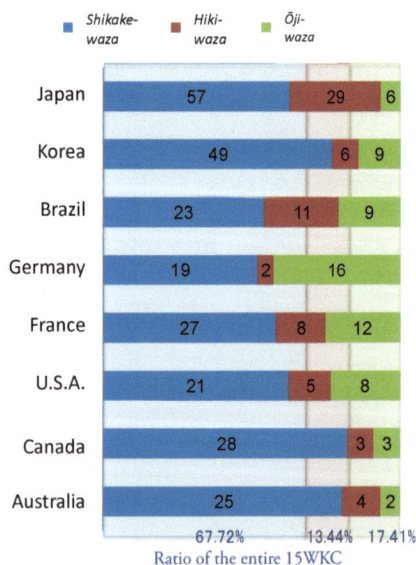

Fig.12. Comparison of the *yūkō-datotsu waza* between the top-ranked countries and the entire women's competition average

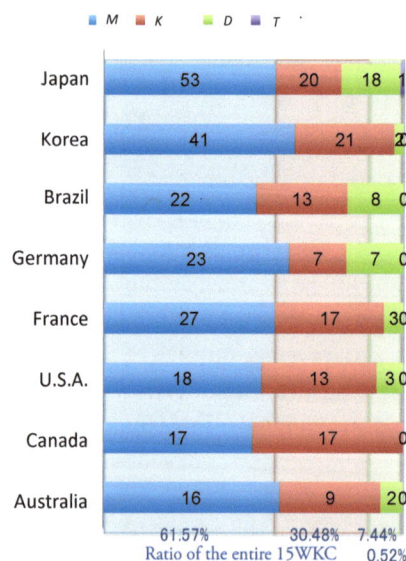

Fig.13. Comparison of the *yūkō-datotsu datotsu-bui* between the top-ranked countries and the entire women's competition average

Table 10. The top-five *waza* used by the top-ranked countries in the women's competition

Countries/Regions	Type of Yuko-datotsu Waza	Yukō-datotsu Scored by the Top-Ranked Countries					
		1st	2nd	3rd	4th	5th	1st
Japan	17	*Men (ippon-uchi)* 20 (21.74%)	*Hiki-men* 14 (15.22%)	*Hiki-dō* 13 (14.13%)	*Debana-men* 12 (13.04%)	*Debana-kote* 11 (11.96%)	
Korea	16	*Men (ippon-uchi)* 14 (21.88%)	*Debana-men* 12 (18.75%)	*Debana-kote*	*Hiki-men* 4 (6.25%)	*Men-men (renzoku-waza)* 3 (4.69%)	*Kote-nuki-men*
Brazil	15	*Debana-kote* 8 (18.60%)	*Hiki-men* 7 (16.28%)	*Debana-men* 5 (11.63%)	*Men (ippon-uchi)* 4	*Hiki-dō* (9.30%)	
Germany	12	*Debana-men* 7	*Debana-kote* (18.92%)	*Men-kaeshi-dō* 6 (16.22%)	*Men-suriage-men (omote)* 4 (10.81%)	*Kote-nuki-men* 3 (8.11%)	
France	12	*Kote-kaeshi-men* 8 (17.02%)	*Men (ippon-uchi)* 7 (14.89%)	*Debana-men*	*Kote (ippon-uchi)* 6 (12.77%)	*Debana-kote*	
U.S.A.	12	*Debana-kote* 10 (29.41%)	*Hiki-men* 5 (14.71%)	*Kote (ippon-uchi)* 3 (8.82%)	*Men-kaeshi-dō*	*Men (ippon-uchi)* / *Harai-men* / *Debana-men* 2 (5.88%)	*Kote-kaeshi-men* / *Kote-uchiotoshi-men*
Canada	11	*Debana-men* 9 (26.47%)	*Kote (ippon-uchi)* 8 (23.53%)	*Debana-kote* 4 (11.76%)	*Men (ippon-uchi)* 3 (8.82%)	*Katsugi-men* / *Hiki-men* / *Kote-nuki-men* 2 (5.88%)	
Australia	12	*Debana-men*	*Debana-kote* 6 (17.65%)	*Men (ippon-uchi)* 5 (14.71%)	*Kote (ippon-uchi)* 2 (5.88%)		

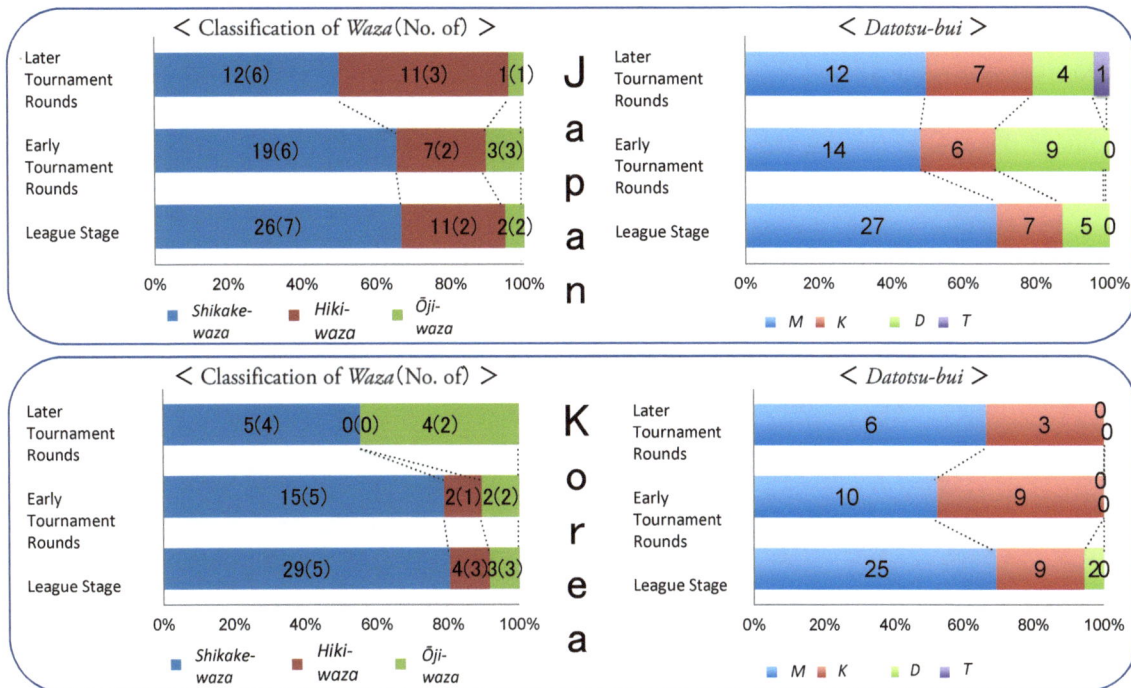

Japan

< Classification of *Waza* (No. of) >

- Later Tournament Rounds: 12(6) | 11(3) | 1(1)
- Early Tournament Rounds: 19(6) | 7(2) | 3(3)
- League Stage: 26(7) | 11(2) | 2(2)

Legend: ■ *Shikake-waza* ■ *Hiki-waza* ■ *Ōji-waza*

< *Datotsu-bui* >

- Later Tournament Rounds: 12 | 7 | 4 | 1
- Early Tournament Rounds: 14 | 6 | 9 | 0
- League Stage: 27 | 7 | 5 | 0

Legend: ■ M ■ K ■ D ■ T

Korea

< Classification of *Waza* (No. of) >

- Later Tournament Rounds: 5(4) | 0(0) | 4(2)
- Early Tournament Rounds: 15(5) | 2(1) | 2(2)
- League Stage: 29(5) | 4(3) | 3(3)

Legend: ■ *Shikake-waza* ■ *Hiki-waza* ■ *Ōji-waza*

< *Datotsu-bui* >

- Later Tournament Rounds: 6 | 3 | 0 | 0
- Early Tournament Rounds: 10 | 9 | 0 | 0
- League Stage: 25 | 9 | 2 | 0

Legend: ■ M ■ K ■ D ■ T

Fig.14. The changes in *waza* used by the finalists in the different stages of the women's competition

kendo in each country is spreading. In the same way as the men's competition, the spread of kendo should not be considered so much by zone but on the basis of each individual country.

3-1-3. Details Regarding the Countries in the Women's Finals

Like the men's, a detailed examination of Japan and Korea is given in Figure 14. The change in *yūkō-datotsu* in matches in the league stage, the early tournament rounds (rounds 1 and 2), and the later tournament rounds (best-16 and above in the individual competition, best-4 and above in the team competition) is shown.

There is only a little data for the later tournament rounds so an exact examination could not be made, but like the men's, it can be said that the *yūkō-datotsu* Japan scored changed as they progressed, unlike Korea. The Japanese women were different to the men in that they used a lot of *hiki-waza*, which could be characteristic of their kendo. It is possible that in an international tournament like the 15WKC, *hiki-waza* could be a tactic used to attain victory.

4. Conclusion

From this study of the aggregate *yūkō-datotsu* seen at the 15WKC, we understood the following points.

1) From all of the *yūkō-datotsu* seen at the 15WKC,

both the men and women used a lot of *shikake-waza* and *men-waza*

2) Comparing the *waza* of the top-ranked countries and regions (across the entire competition)
- Classification of *waza*:
  ▶ Many *hiki-waza*: Japan, Brazil
  ▶ Many *ōji-waza*: U.S.A., France
- *Datotsu-bui*:
  ▶ Many *men*: Korea
  ▶ Many *dō*: Japan

- The change of the finalists as they progressed in the competition
  ▶ Japan: Both the men and women scored various *yūkō-datotsu*. As the competition progressed to later stages, the ratio changed.
  ▶ Korea: Both the men and women scored many *men-waza*, made up mainly by *shikake-waza*. That ratio was not affected as the competition progressed but was fairly consistent throughout.

3) Comparison with the men's and women's All Japan Kendo Championships (2012, 2013)
- Classification of *waza*: The men used a lot of *hiki-waza*, a little *ōji-waza*. The women were almost the same.
- *Datotsu-bui*: The men scored many *men* and a few *kote*. The women scored a few *men* and many *kote*.

The WKC in Graphs

Text by Michael Ishimatsu-Prime and Yulin Zhuang
Graphs by Yulin Zhuang

The 16th World Kendo Championship is the fourth to be held in Japan, and the second time that the Nippon Budokan will serve as the venue. This is also the first WKC location decided by the bid system rather than by rotation within the Asia, Europe, and America zones. From here on, much like the Olympic Games and the FIFA World Cup, the host nation for each subsequent WKC will be decided through the bidding system. Maybe the Nippon Budokan will once again serve as the venue in the future. If it does, it will probably look a little different as it is due to undergo a major refurbishment in preparation for the 2020 Tokyo Olympic Games where it will once again be the judo venue.

In the 45 years since the Budokan held the 1st WKC, the kendo world has changed considerably. There has been steady growth in kendo and there are now more countries and people practising kendo than ever before. Fig. 1 illustrates kendo's growth with regards to participation in the WKC in terms of participants and federations. At the 1st WKC there were 144 competi-tors and officials from 17 federations. For the 16th WKC there are 56 federations registered to compete. That is almost a 325% increase. However, there has been even greater growth—about 600%—in the number of competitors and officials, to a staggering 856. Kendo has been increasing in popularity worldwide which explains some of this increase. However, a great deal of the increase in participants can be attributed to the inclusion of a women's competition. The first women's WKC tournament was held in 1997 in Kyoto. The women's competition reached its current format in 2000 and became official in 2003 in Glasgow, but more about the women later.

Aside from a few blips in 1973, 1988, 1997 and 2009, the number of participants has been steadily increasing. Participation numbers had their two biggest increases in 2012 and 2015. The downtick and subsequent increase for the 14th WKC in 2009 (Brazil) and the 15th WKC in 2012 (Italy) can possibly be attributed to the hefty travel expenses to get to Brazil for the majority of competitors.

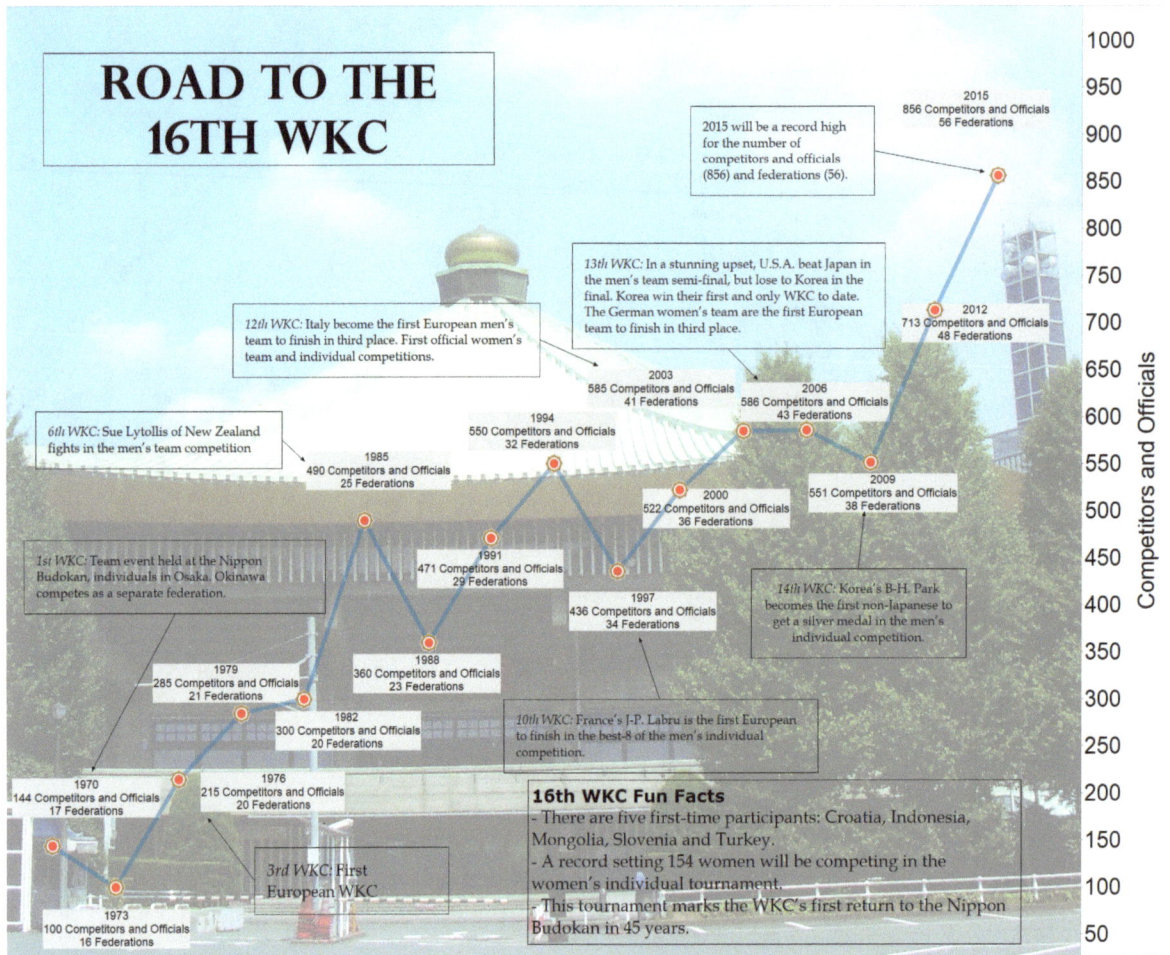

Fig. 1—The Road to the 16th WKC graph showing the increase in participants over time. Milestones and participation figures are also indicated.

Fig. 2—1st to Best-8 Men's and Women's Team and Individual results since the 11th WKC in 2000.

The WKC in Graphs

There was also a massive increase in the number of participating competitors and officials, the biggest ever, from the 1982 to 1985 WKCs. In fact, it took nearly a decade for the WKC to surpass that number.

This year sees five federations make their debut: Croatia, Indonesia, Mongolia, Slovenia, and Turkey. This ties with the 15th WKC in Italy as the highest number of debutants. Ecuador, Latvia, Lithuania, Montenegro, and Serbia took their bow in 2012. Together, the new participants in these two WKC represent nearly a fifth of the entire number. In fact, Aruba is the only federation registered with the FIK that will not be in attendance at the 16th WKC.

Since the inception of the WKC in 1970 only the federations from Australia, Brazil, Canada, France, Great Britain, Hawaii, Japan, Korea, Sweden, Switzerland, and the U.S.A. have competed in every event.

Like every other WKC, Japan will be the favourites again in Tokyo. With one exception, a shock third-place men's team finish in 2006, Japan has dominated the winner's podium in every category. A look at Fig. 2 shows their historical primacy.

Fig. 2 shows the best-8 positions for the men's and women's team and individual competitions since the 11th WKC in Santa Clara, 2000. Prior to this, there were several variations in the tournament structure that make comparison difficult. For example, at the 10th WKC in Kyoto in 1997, there were two men's team divisions, I and II. Also, the women's team competition allowed more than one team per federation, and the women's individual competition had a 2-dan-and-under as well as a 3-dan-and-over competition. Furthermore, in some of the early WKCs, there was not actually a best-8 group.

Since 2000 in the men's team competition, with the exception of 2006 and 2009, it has been a Japan/Korea final, with the U.S.A. managing to break in a few times. The Japanese women have a spotless record, but there has been slightly more variation in the finalists with Brazil also managing a 2nd place finish.

When we look at the men's semi-finalists, there have been a total of eight different countries making it to that stage since the 11th WKC: Brazil, Canada, Chinese Taipei, Hungary, Italy, Japan, Korea, and the U.S.A. If the quarter-final finishers are included, there are a total of 17 with Australia, Belgium, France, Germany, Great Britain, New Zealand, Spain, Sweden, and Switzerland joining the semi-finalists.

In the women's team competition there have been seven different representatives at the quarter-final stage: Brazil, Canada, Chinese Taipei, Germany, Japan, Korea, and the U.S.A. In addition to these countries, the women's team quarter-finalists also feature Australia, France, Finland, Hungary, and Italy, making a total of 12 different countries to make it to the best-8 stage.

From this we can see that the men's team competition has had more variation at the quarter-final stage, with about 50% more countries. However, it should be noted that there is far greater participation in the men's team competition than the women's. At the 11th WKC there were 30 men's teams/19 women's teams; 12th WKC, 36/20; 13th WKC, 39/21; 14th WKC, 34/19; 15th WKC, 47/30.

The Japanese women in the individual competition have been far more dominant than their male compatriots in the individual competition, taking all top four spots, except in 2009 when Brazilian Eliete Takashina dared to challenge their superiority with a semi-finalist finish. Kate Sylvester alludes to the reason for this dominance in her article in this edition of *Kendo World*.

A Japanese man has won all of the men's individual titles, but the Koreans have been making their presence felt in the top four in the past few years, particularly in 2009 when Korean kendoka finished second and took both of the semi-finalist positions.

In the men's individual competition, in addition to Japan and Korea, competitors from Australia, Belgium, Canada, Chinese Taipei, Finland, France, and the U.S.A. have made it to the quarter-final stage—a total of nine different nationalities. In the women's individual competition, the Brazilian and Japanese semi-finalists have been joined by kenshi from Canada, Finland, France, Hungary, Italy, Korea, and the U.S.A. in the quarter-finals making, like the men, nine different nationalities in the quarter-finals.

The WKC in Graphs

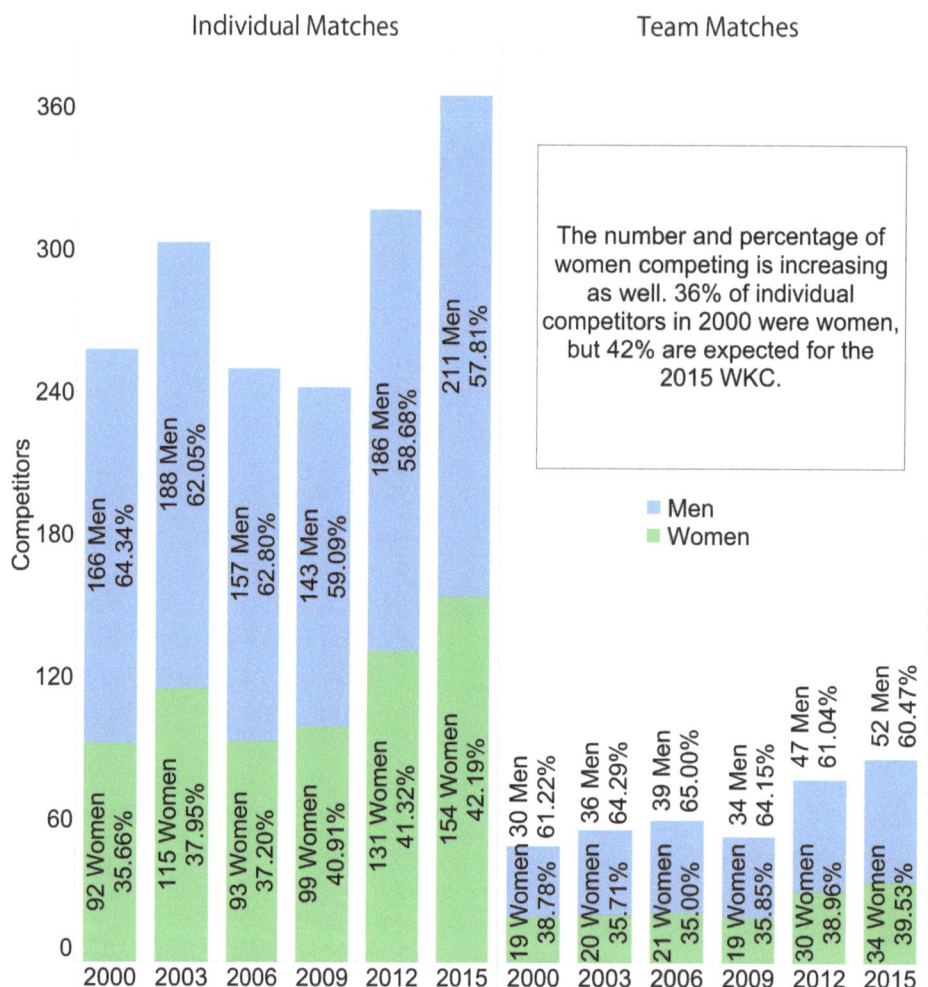

Fig.3—The number of male and female competitors in the individual and team competitions since the 11th WKC in 2000.

The mobility in the number of best-8 finishers is an encouraging sign for the internationalisation of kendo, as strong competitors and teams are cropping up in more and more countries. Long-time participants such as the U.S.A., Great Britain, and France cannot rest secure, and must keep an open eye on the up-and-coming new federations. Perhaps this year will see Japan defeated on its home turf and usher in a new era of competition. Or, Japan may maintain its primacy and provide an inspiring role model to all participating kenshi.

Fig. 3 shows the percentage of male and female competitors in both the team and individual competitions since the 11th WKC in 2000. It is

encouraging to note that in both the team and individual competitions since the 13th WKC (Taipei, 2006), the percentage of women has been steadily increasing making the balance more even. This year marks a high in both the absolute number of female competitors and the percentage.

It will be interesting to see what the make-up of federations and competitors will be in Korea in 2018, and if that WKC will see the same sort of growth as the 16th WKC. With the continued increase in the number of women in the WKC, together with the total number of federations and competitors, the future of world kendo is looking bright.

The Kendo World WKC Guess Who!

Do you know who these people are? Do you want to win a pair of original Kendo World *kote*? If the answer to both of these questions is "Yes", then enter this competition! Five Zinio eBook editions of Kendo World are also up for grabs!*

Here is a selection of programme mug shots of some well-known competitors in WKC history, along with some dazzling retro hairstyles. Some of the photos even date back to the 1967 World Goodwill Kendo Match, the competition that preceded the WKC. If you recognise these competitors, send an email with their names and corresponding numbers to guesswho@kendo-world.com.

If you don't know them all, you could still be in with a chance. If no one guesses everyone in this stunning array of kendo celebs, whoever gets the most right will become the proud owner of a pair of Kendo World's exclusive *kote*. And there's more! Five people will receive a Zinio eBook edition of Kendo World. If more than one person guesses all the names correctly, the winner will be drawn from a hat.

So, what are you waiting for? You could be the next kendowiki champ!

* In order to receive a Zinio edition of Kendo World, a valid Zinio account is needed. See www.zinio.com for details.
** Entries must be received by July 31, 2015.
*** Only one entry per person.

1   2   3   4   5

6   7   8   9   10

11   12   13   14   15

16   17   18   19   20

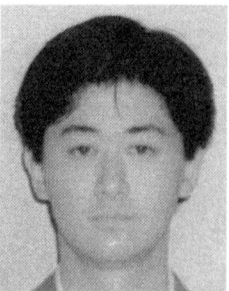

21   22   23   24   25

26

27

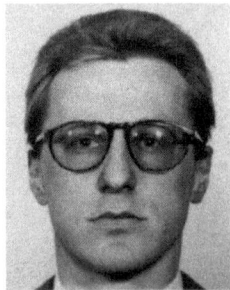

28

29

30

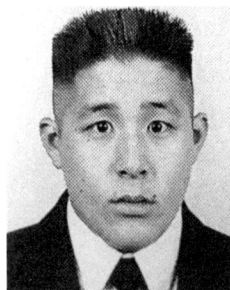

31

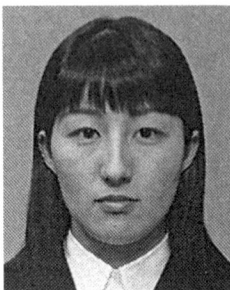

32

33

34

35

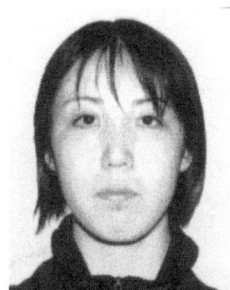

36

37

38

39

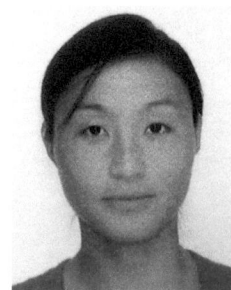

40

41

42

43

44

45

46

47

48

49

50

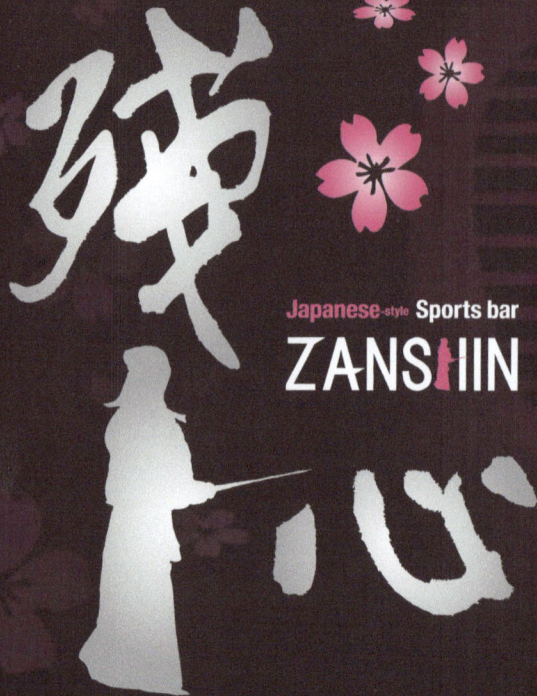

国際武道大学

INTERNATIONAL BUDO UNIVERSITY

Budo Specialization Program